Domicide

Domicide
Architecture, War and the Destruction of Home in Syria

AMMAR AZZOUZ

BLOOMSBURY VISUAL ARTS
LONDON • NEW YORK • OXFORD • NEW DELHI • SYDNEY

BLOOMSBURY VISUAL ARTS
Bloomsbury Publishing Plc
50 Bedford Square, London, WC1B 3DP, UK
1385 Broadway, New York, NY 10018, USA
29 Earlsfort Terrace, Dublin 2, Ireland

BLOOMSBURY, BLOOMSBURY VISUAL ARTS and the Diana logo are trademarks of
Bloomsbury Publishing Plc

First published in Great Britain 2023
Paperback edition published 2025

Copyright © Ammar Azzouz, 2025

Ammar Azzouz has asserted his right under the Copyright, Designs and Patents Act,
1988, to be identified as Author of this work.

For legal purposes the Acknowledgements on p. xviii constitute an extension
of this copyright page.

Cover design by Eleanor Rose
Cover image: The Destruction of the City of Homs, 2016, Deanna Petherbridge CBE, Tate
London, courtesy of the artist

All rights reserved. No part of this publication may be reproduced or transmitted
in any form or by any means, electronic or mechanical, including photocopying,
recording, or any information storage or retrieval system, without prior
permission in writing from the publishers.

Bloomsbury Publishing Plc does not have any control over, or responsibility for, any
third-party websites referred to or in this book. All internet addresses given in
this book were correct at the time of going to press. The author and publisher
regret any inconvenience caused if addresses have changed or sites have
ceased to exist, but can accept no responsibility for any such changes.

A catalogue record for this book is available from the British Library.

A catalog record for this book is available from the Library of Congress.

ISBN: HB: 978-1-3502-4810-6
      PB: 978-1-3502-4814-4
      ePDF: 978-1-3502-4811-3
      eBook: 978-1-3502-4812-0

Typeset by RefineCatch Limited, Bungay, Suffolk
Printed and bound in Great Britain

To find out more about our authors and books visit www.bloomsbury.com
and sign up for our newsletters.

13.5 million.
And more.

Contents

List of illustrations ix
Preface xi
Foreword *by Lyse Doucet* xiii
Acknowledgements xviii

Introduction 1

The domicide question 1
War on the city 6
Domicide: The destruction of home 14
Extreme and everyday domicide 18
Wartime domicide 19
'Peacetime' domicide 20
Writing Syria from afar 22
The argument 25

1 Domicide: Slow violence, division and destruction 29

Space of identity 30
Space of inequality 36
Widening gap between architects and communities 41
Space of protests 44
Space of war 49
Space of alienation 52
Conclusions 53

2 War on home: In search of a place to call home 55

Loss of home 56
In search of home 59
Impact of internal displacement on people 61
Responses to destruction 69
Charities as a collective act of solidarity 71

Architects at the time of war 73
'Everyone is an architect' 75
Conclusions 76

3 Domicide and representation 79
Syria in exile 79
Artists' responses to domicide 89
Deanna Petherbridge: On domicide of Homs 92
Conclusions 95

4 Domicidal reconstruction 97
Emerging debates on Syria's future reconstruction 100
Dilemmas of reconstruction 104
Reconstruction for the chosen few 108
Reconstruction as a weapon 113
Reconstructing cultural heritage 117
Conclusions 122

5 Domicide in war and peace 125
'We are still here' 125
Resisting domicide: Reclaiming our narrative 127
Collective spaces of solidarity 131
Protecting memory 134
Violence at home 135

Bibliography 137
Index 151

Illustrations

Figures

Intro.1 Destruction of Masha' al-Arb'een, Hama, (*a*) 2008 and (*b*) 2019. Google Earth   4
Intro.2 Benghazi city centre, 2018. Nada Elfeituri   7
Intro.3 Mousawarah, (*a*) 2015, (*b*) 2017 and (*c*) 2019. Google Earth   21
1.1 One of the remaining old buildings in Homs (*bottom left*), just outside the walled city of Homs, 2009. Ammar Azzouz   32
1.2 (*a*) Significant parts of the Old City of Homs were demolished in the early 1980s. (*b*) Remains of its wall still stand in these demolished areas, 2009. Ammar Azzouz   33
1.3 The Clock Tower Square, Homs, 2010. Ammar Azzouz   45
1.4 Women protesting in Homs, 31 October 2011. Given to the author with a request for anonymity   46
2.1 Families march to the Old City of Homs after the end of its siege, 2014. Omama Zankawan, taken by S.Z.   63
2.2 A scene from the Old City of Homs after the end of its siege, 2014. Omama Zankawan, taken by S.Z.   64
2.3 A woman and a child walking in the Old City of Homs, 2014. Omama Zankawan, taken by S.Z.   65
2.4 Omama in her grandparents' flat in Homs, 2014. Omama Zankawan, taken by S.Z.   66
3.1(*a*) Homs Clock Tower at Homsi House in London, 2021. Sana Kikhia   82
3.1(*b*) A replica of the New Clock Tower in a refugee camp in Greece, 2016. Katie Wong   82
3.2 Coventry Cathedral, 1962. Arup   86
3.3 *31 Days in the Capital of the Revolution*, 2014. Tiffany Chung   90
3.4 ISW: areas of control; UNHCR: numbers and locations of Syrian refugees and IDPs as of April 2019; 2019. Tiffany Chung   92
3.5 *The Destruction of the City of Homs*, 2016. Deanna Petherbridge. Courtesy of the artist. Photographer: John Bodkin   94
3.6 *The Destruction of Palmyra*, 2017. Deanna Petherbridge. Courtesy of the artist. Photographer: Stephen White   94

4.1	*Weaponized Urbanism*, 2019. Aliaa Aboukhaddour, Yasmeen Fanari for aljumhuriya.net (2019)	105
4.2	*Weaponized Urbanism*, 2019. Aliaa Aboukhaddour, Yasmeen Fanari for aljumhuriya.net (2019)	105
4.3	(*a*) Basateen El-Razi, 2012 and (*b*) 2019. Google Earth	111
4.4	Damage to the Khalid ibn al-Walid Mosque, 2014 (*a*) and (*b*). Omama Zankawan, taken by S.Z.	117

Boxes

2.1	Omama's story of displacement and domicide, 2021	62
2.2	Hanan's story of displacement and domicide, 2021	66
4.1	Reflections on the future reconstruction	100

Preface

I recall a day that will never be erased from my mind: 16 October 2011. Peaceful demonstrators were marching in Homs, Syria. It was soon targeted. My friend, Taher Al Sebai, an architecture student was killed. Two other children were killed too. It was the first time I had lost someone since the start of the Revolution in Syria in March 2011. But it was not the last. Tanks were already in the streets of the Baba Amr neighbourhood when I marched with hundreds of Homsis to bury my friend Taher. Snipers were already taking their positions on tower blocks. Each day was a struggle to survive, would I be next? – I often asked. One by one, we started losing people too young to die. The days of youth that were supposed to be filled with joy, hopes and dreams were the days of loss, grief and trauma. People who imagined a future where they could live in dignity, freedom and justice started to see their dreams being crushed. Only a month after the loss of my friend, I left for the UK on 17 November 2011.

I have never returned since then. For over a decade in Syria now, millions of people have been living in a damaged world. We stand on the ruins of a world that once was. The human condition of millions of Syrians has been shaped by different types of pain, with repeated damage, harm, rupture, loss and violence all through time.

The questions of home and its destruction, domicide, are hence personal to me. I arrived in the UK in 2011 with two bags, starting my life from scratch in a new city and separated from my family and friends, without being able to meet them or to visit my home city. From miles away, I have seen my country being destroyed and suffered the trauma from being unable to return, unable to be with the people who needed me when they were suffering. I have seen the people I love in pain and despair, struggling to find a clinic for their illnesses, unable to get the weekly bread they need, and losing their homes and family members. I have seen them in pain each day, and this pain has also been mine. I have collapsed many times after phone calls with people in Homs. The challenges they face each day, the misery they live in, their struggle to access their basic needs of electricity, water and food continue to shape their everyday life today, over a decade since the start of the revolution.

In exile, it felt as if my life was split into two: one in the comfort of London where I currently reside, and another in Homs where I was born and raised.

Images of the ruined homes and damaged lives have never left my mind. Seeing the war from afar made me struggle to put down roots, to quest for a sense of belonging in my own exile. I failed many times to put the struggle into words, because words are inadequate in the face of the pain we have endured. I saw the people in Homs living in the practice of waiting, dying slowly on each passing day. The pain has been unbearable that even after more than ten years into the conflict, signs of hope are difficult to capture. Those who live in the war zone are suffering tremendously. The suffering continues in different ways for Syrians who came as refugees and now reside in cities such as Amman, Beirut, Istanbul and Berlin. I have seen the exiled Syrians in pain, wounded and traumatized, struggling to reconstruct a new home. This is why I wish in this book to focus not only on those who remain in Syria, but also on those who left the country in their quest to rebuild their shattered lives.

Although I have been away from Syria for over a decade now without being able to return, I felt a sense of responsibility to do something: to tell our story of a forgotten war. The narrative about Syria has been damaged and redirected. We have to preserve the narrative, to tell the story. We have to fight to remember. In words, I have found a refuge in my isolating exile, and I have found a tool to resist domicide. In words, I have found a shelter, a home, in hopes that these words will be read and make a change. As Syrians have gradually been turned into numbers by international organizations and newspapers when they report on us, I started talking to people in Homs and to write about their everyday lives so as to individualize the human suffering in war zones and to resist the transformation of our suffering into digits (Azzouz 2018, 2019, 2020c). But I am not alone in doing so. Syrians, their friends and allies across the world are working on different fronts through their art, literature, activism, music, education and culture. My work is only a small contribution towards the collective work that Syrians and their allies are doing across different corners of the world to resist domicide. I dedicate it to the people of Syria.

Foreword

'I am making a short trip but promise I will get to your foreword as soon as possible,' I reassured Ammar Azzouz in an email on 20 February 2022 as I headed back to the Ukrainian capital Kyiv in the midst of an intensifying speculation: would Russia's President Vladimir Putin really send his tanks and troops across Ukraine's border? Ammar's reply to my message arrived on 3 March, about a week after Russia unleashed its devastating onslaught: 'all the images make the memory of Syria flood my mind . . .'

All the images were tumbling into our lives again. Moscow's cruise missiles smashing into high-rise residential blocks, exposing wrecked homes within: tidy rooms turned topsy-turvy; crockery shattered; children's torn toys strewn across the floor. Heartbreaking images of petite suburban bungalows with pocket gardens swallowed up by flames. Stomach-churning images of bodies sprawled out along the streets.

Not long after Ammar's message, I heard much the same from Ukraine's deputy mayor, Sergei Orlov, from the southern city of Mariupol: 'look at the photos of Aleppo, this is Mariupol today.' Aleppo, the ancient metropolis of northern Syria, pounded for years by Russian and Syrian warplanes until December 2016 when rebel fighters in the shredded streets in the city's east finally surrendered. In early 2022, the target was Mariupol, an industrial hub on the shores of the Sea of Azov, blasted into a wasteland of smouldering ruins as Russian firepower bombed and besieged the city into submission.

This is what makes Azzouz's scholarly work ever more essential, and urgent. Wars of our time, sometimes fought in our name, are not in the trenches; they're fought street-to-street, house-to-house, one home after another. Why does a hospital, a kindergarten, always seem to be hit in every outbreak of hostilities? After nearly four decades of reporting on conflict, I now often say: civilians are not close to the front lines; they are the front line.

In Syria and Ukraine, and wars before and beyond, this kind of destruction has often been called 'collateral damage', or civilians 'caught in the crossfire' – the kind of language which can sanitize, even be used to excuse, potential war crimes. As Azzouz so powerfully explores in this book, this is domicide: the deliberate destruction of home, causing suffering to its people. To use even more brutal language, it is the 'murder of homes and ways of life' (Catterall: 2014: 385).

And it is not just a matter of major military operations. Azzouz's book begins with an example of the more everyday, less noticed, stripping away of rights and belongings. In July 2013, a fire swept through the City Council in the Syrian city of Homs. But it was no ordinary fire. The blaze destroyed the Housing Land and Property records to, in Azzouz's words, 'erase people from the pages of land and property documents'. It was an attack by bureaucrats, not bombs and bullets. It is what Azzouz calls 'the interconnection between everyday and extreme domicide'. Its impact cuts deep, very deep.

I first met Azzouz in January 2017, when the American Embassy in London hosted an exhibition entitled *The Art of Resilience*. Bright white walls, normally reserved for framed photographs of the long line of US ambassadors, gave pride of place to the powerful, provocative, work of five Syrian artists. Azzouz was one of them, a young architecture student working on his PhD at the University of Bath, UK. To draw a smile from his shy demeanour, I teased him that he had subconsciously chosen Bath because of its echo of the ruling Ba'ath Party of Syria; its repressive rule dominated every life in Syria, including giving its name to Al-Baath University where Azzouz first studied. War's black humour. We exchanged knowing smiles; it started our conversation which continues to this day.

Azzouz's drawings, in sharp lines of black ink, were unsettling. Invisible wounds of war – loss and trauma – laid bare. Distorted faces of individuals were emotional maps: homes lost by forced exile or ferocious fighting; memories stolen as entire streets were reduced to rubble; precious centuries-old ancestry now just dust. A geography of grief transposed into lifeblood of aching, unremitting pain.

I had just returned from Aleppo, the city described as one of the world's oldest continuously inhabited cities. A bloody chapter in its storied history had just ended. The forces of Syria's president, Bashar al-Assad, backed by powerful friends Russia and Iran, had finally seized this prize, the last major urban area which had been partially and briefly captured by a range of rebel forces linked to an array of allies, including Western powers, Arab states, Türkiye, as well as extremist groups such as Al-Qaeda.

In 2016, Aleppo had been the symbol of Syria's suffering, the world's badge of honour to do something to stop it. In December that year, the US Ambassador to the UN, Samantha Power, told the Security Council that Aleppo would stand as an event in world history, like other atrocities, 'that define modern evil, that stain our conscience decades later'. The victory of the Syrian government, and its allies, marked a major turning point in this brutal conflict; it also marked the moment when Syria started slipping away from the world's gaze.

When Syria first shot into our headlines in the spring of 2011, it was Azzouz's hometown, Homs in western Syria, which came to be known as 'the capital of the revolution'. These were the first heady months of unprecedented uprisings, arrestingly labelled as the 'Arab Spring'. Peaceful protests unseated presidents for life in Tunisia and Egypt, and spread to the towns and cities of Libya, Yemen and more, including Syria. In places like Homs, demonstrations courageously held in the streets of an authoritarian state dazzled many around the world. But they soon morphed into some of the bloodiest battles challenging the decades-long grip of the Assad family.

We hear little now of Syria's war, not much of Libya's and Yemen's humanitarian disaster only rarely flickers into our daily news – whether we digest it from television or radio sets, computers or telephones. Even now as I write this, six months into the Ukraine War, we hear of 'war fatigue'. In some ways, this is not surprising. Our own lives, other crises, eclipse what can seem to be distant disasters. Conflicts often take different shapes after the shock of their early days and months. They – sadly – evolve into a more 'normal' kind of crisis which only occasionally beeps on the radars of politicians, journalists, human rights organizations and in our own lives.

But these wars live on, especially in the lives of those who cannot escape them. My friendship with Azzouz continues to remind me of this. When I attend graduation ceremonies, and celebrate with students, I remember his painful account of how his parents could only join his graduation from the University of Bath by video. They cannot come to England; he cannot return to Syria. On another occasion, at a literary festival, that kind of place where many of us retreat into a joyful appreciation of books, Azzouz and I once shared a panel. He spoke of seeing a couple walking in the park with their son. This simple scene of a child with his parents caused him to collapse in tears. Something so ordinary was now, unbearably, beyond reach. It is the story of so very many severed from their loved ones, their homeland, their homes.

This goes beyond individual emotions, as important as they are. I have also benefitted enormously from attending seminars and events organized by, among others, Arup, an international firm working on different disciplines of the built environment (where Ammar worked), and the Heritage Network at the University of Oxford (where Azzouz is now a Research Fellow), where scholars are conducting more systematic research into this destruction, and reconstruction, of cities. Azzouz's own research underscores how this work must not only draw on maps, documents and photographs. It is the amalgams of individual memories, writ large, which can provide compelling evidence of systematic efforts to destroy personal attachments, erase identity of entire streets and cities and engineer new ones.

When journalists write their 'first rough draft of history', we sometimes see snippets of these individual stories, often recorded in the immediate shock of an attack, a death, an immense loss. Sometimes these small stories are also written in broad brush strokes. In Aleppo, for example, the boundaries between the rebel-held east and government-controlled west of the city were sometimes blurred in the media. In Homs, the besieged ancient quarter, or very distinct embattled neighbourhoods, with their own histories and character, were sometimes just known as Homs.

There is, too, as Azzouz points out, a tendency to focus on monumental and ancient heritage. Aleppo first appeared in our headlines in September 2012 when parts of its storied souk, 700 years of history, went up in flames during the fighting between government and rebel forces. It set alarm bells ringing around the world, and rightly so. But there was not the space, or indeed the access, to tell the stories of the countless homes and lives which also went up in smoke. When I visited Syria's stunning Roman ruins in Palmyra in 2017, after Syrian government forces pushed out Islamic State (IS) fighters, I was surprised to see there was an adjacent town, also called Palmyra, which had suffered enormously during the repressive rule of IS. It had received almost no mention.

Sometimes documentaries return to the same streets, the same people, to tell more in-depth stories of wars which ended or still go on. But the consequences of conflicts reverberate for generations and demand more nuanced understandings of what has gone before: for more sensitive reconstruction efforts by major aid agencies; for more empathetic refugee programmes. And lasting peace can only be won if there is also justice, a reckoning, a strong signal that war crimes and crimes against humanity will not go unpunished. That requires proof of what really happened.

Consider, for example, the war in Ukraine. Russia, like most warring powers, insists it does not target civilians. There can of course be errant missiles which strike wide of the mark. Civilian infrastructure sometimes shields military hardware. But in Ukraine, there was a sinister pattern to Russia's deadly attacks. As the UN's High Commissioner for Human Rights Michelle Bachelet bluntly put it, 'The massive destruction of civilian objects and the high number of civilian casualties strongly indicate that the fundamental principles of distinction, proportionality and precaution have not been sufficiently adhered to.'

Even wars have rules; the rules of war are enshrined in the Geneva Conventions. And in the proverbial fog of war, no one can claim the moral high ground. A comprehensive investigation carried out by the *New York Times* into American airstrikes against the Taliban and other armed groups in Afghanistan, waged with precision bombs and all-seeing drones, revealed a pattern of 'flawed intelligence, faulty targeting, years of civilian deaths, and scant accountability'. Azzouz points to the city of Raqqa, the US example in Syria, now 'synonymous with ruins and urban misery'. Furthermore, Raqqa was occupied by extremist Islamic State fighters. Between June and October 2017, it came under intense bombardment by the US-led Global Coalition which also included UK and French forces. It may be argued that stark differences in war aims, in the scale and scope of operations, puts these examples in different categories. But their end result is the same – homes are smashed, lives shattered and lost. Why, Azzouz asks, has no current academic research focused on the city of Raqqa, and its destruction?

This book also highlights another essential aspect of our understanding, not just of the research which must be done but also of how it is done and who does it. In many realms, from journalism to academe to literature and art, there is now a deepening appreciation that whoever asks the questions and seeks the answers can have a decisive impact on how much, and what kind of, knowledge we gain. A new generation of scholars, researchers and writers bring to their work a fluency in relevant languages and a more visceral understanding of their own cultures and societies, including its deepest pain and greatest joys. This is lived experience. Combined with the ability to stand back with a scholar's skills, and dig deeper with a researcher's rigour, books like Azzouz's can help us reach a new understanding of what is, arguably, one of the most evocative, most important, words in the English language: home. Its meaning matters to all of us – especially when it is ripped away.

Lyse Doucet
BBC Chief International Correspondent
London, July 2022

Acknowledgements

This book has been researched and written over a period of almost five years in the early mornings and during weekends whilst working full time. Across these years, I have had conversations with many people through panel discussions, webinars, conferences and lectures. I owe my gratitude to many Syrian friends and colleagues and to the people whom I met for standing in solidarity with the Syrian people and with Syria.

I am deeply grateful to the wonderful Bloomsbury team for giving me this opportunity to write my first academic book and for their editorial suggestions on the manuscript. Thank you Alexander Highfield, Rosamunde O'Cleirigh and James Thompson for believing in me from the early days when we met in Bloomsbury, London, just before the pandemic.

I am grateful to Professor Heather Viles and Dr Alex Vasudevan for giving me incredible support during my time at the School of Geography and the Environment at the University of Oxford. Before I started writing, I reached out to several academics, seeking their advice on writing my first academic book so I could learn from their experiences. I am thankful for Professor Dawn Chatty and Dr Sarah Fine for their insights and suggestions.

The book has benefitted from critical feedback and insights from several colleagues and friends who read different chapters, including artist and dear friend Deanna Petherbridge, architect Lama Sulaiman and scholar, activist and friend Noura Aljizawi. I wish to thank Dr Yunpeng Zhang whom I have admired for his work on domicide in China. Dr Zhang generously read most of the book and provided precious feedback whilst suggesting areas for improvement and clarifications. Dr Omnia Khalil kindly reviewed the structure of my book and gave me her feedback and suggestions as I learned from her great work on Egypt.

My writing has been shaped by the moves I had to make. I first wrote in Belsize Park in North-West London, then in Bloomsbury in Central London. I then moved to Ancoats in Manchester and then returned to North-West London where I lived in Kentish Town. So, as I was writing about home, I was myself moving homes. I have written this book in a personal capacity and in my private time. I was able to schedule my day to prepare the book and would wake up at five in the morning before starting my working hours at nine. The

ACKNOWLEDGEMENTS

evenings were spent mostly reading. I am grateful to Arup for awarding me a small grant to spend a number of days writing. At Arup, I would like to thank all of my friends and colleagues who provided endless encouragement during my work there between 2017 and 2022; especially, the endless kindness, solidarity and warmth of Padraig Coakley.

In Homs, many people have been incredible and generous with their time. This book is for them, and it would not have been possible without them. Outside of Homs, many people in the diaspora have kept Homs in their hearts. I am so thankful to many Homsis in exile who shared their knowledge and experiences with me, including Omama Zankawan, Wael Rihani and Sana Kikhia. I am also grateful to the wonderful Lyse Doucet, who has been a great inspiration throughout the years. Her work has brought millions of people close to the everyday lives of civilians in conflict situations. Her kindness has brought so much hope to me in some of the darkest moments.

I am thankful to my family, to my friends, Susanna, Nerida, Khaldia, Thomas and Mahivi, and my beloved ones, Dr Alaa Droubi and Dr Mario Ausseloos, for their endless love, friendship, kindness and care. They made this life less painful and more beautiful.

Ammar Azzouz
London, July 2022.

Introduction

The domicide question

On 1 July 2013, a short video emerged showing fire and flames spreading across the City Council in Homs, Syria. The fire had spread across one of the top floors, whilst flames started travelling upwards. To the communities in Homs, and in a city where over half of the neighbourhoods have been badly destroyed in the past decade, this was more than the burning of a building. The building, which is situated in the heart of the Old City of Homs, contains the Housing, Land and Property (HLP) records of the city. For Homsi communities, regardless of how, why, who and when all of this happened, it was a threat to their presence in the city, an erasure of their documents and records. Scholars, writers and activists have accused the Syrian government of deliberately targeting the building. It was the only structure burned down in one of the secure parts of the city (Unruh 2016). The Syrian government rejected these accusations, whilst noting that the HLP records were safe in new offices to which they were moved.

With the mass destruction of people's homes during the past decade and the threats against their ownership records, architecture has been weaponized to provide legitimacy, power and sovereignty. The deliberate targeting of HLP records has been seen as a tool to re-engineer the demography in Homs, replacing the opposing communities to the regime with those who support it based on sectarian and political lines (Al-Homsi 2013). As Jihad Yazigi, the founder and editor of *The Syria Report*, notes: 'the destruction of records not only prevents the original owners from reclaiming their property, but also allows the transfer of the property to pro-regime individuals and groups' (2017: 6). Reports show that there has been a replacement of people who lived in certain parts of the country with other people from Syria, as well as with loyalists to the regime from Lebanon, Iraq and Iran (Chulov 2017).

But it was not only Homs that witnessed the destruction of its HLP records. Offices were confirmed to have been burnt in Zabadani, Darayya and Qusayr, which was besieged by Hezbollah, a Lebanese Shia Islamist political party and militant group, in early 2013 (Chulov 2017). Seven years after the burning of the City Hall in Homs, a 'leak' was recorded in the building of the HLP records in Salamiyah in February 2020. A video released by the Syrian TV showed staff members putting damaged, wet and worn documents in the open air in an attempt to dry them in a chaotic scene of despair (Radio and TV Station in Hama 2020). One of the staff members who was interviewed noted that they hoped to digitize these documents once they are dry, showing the urgent need to have an online platform to supplement the hard copies of these records: to protect the rights of people. This was not the end. More recently, in September 2021, another building was burning. It was the HLP records building in Hama, a city that is fully under the control of the government. These multiple and repeated cases have raised concerns about the government's attempts to dispossess forcibly displaced people of their properties if they were unable to provide their ownership documents.

With over 13.5 million Syrians displaced from their homes, both inside and outside Syria, making up half of the Syrian population, there are fears about their right to return, including major concerns about their HLP rights. Reports have already shown the use of forged documents to carry out the sale and transfer of people's homes to new owners (Nassar 2021). Illegal HLP transactions threaten the future return of displaced people. Challenges will emerge in tracing their records or determining superiority over the multiple competing claims to the same property (Norwegian Refugee Council 2016). The loss of HLP documents and the targeting of HLP archives might weaken the claims over HLP assets by their original owners and lay the foundation for the occupation and/or the transfer of these assets to other individuals or reconstruction companies.

During the war and conflict, new laws and decrees have emerged turning such concerns about HLP rights into realities of destruction, dispossession and displacement. One of the most controversial ones is Law 10, which was passed in March 2018. On enacting the law, the government gave only thirty days for HLP owners to provide proof of ownership. The law has caused local and international outrage as it was seen as a tool to further punish forcibly displaced communities who fled their homes, who, in many cases, did so without taking their HLP records with them. The Syrian government passed another law, Law 42, to extend the deadline to one year. But concerns remained and fears grew, as Law 10 is considered 'a tool for the dispossession of those Syrians who cannot prove their ownership due to their political convictions or activism' (Said and Yazigi 2018). Whilst bombs and shells have been falling all over the country and causing mass destruction, a war of a different kind was going on through new urban planning laws and decrees over people's homes and lands.

As a response to the attacks on HLP records, efforts have been directed towards safeguarding official documents of refugees and Internally Displaced

Persons (IDPs). The Day After (TDA), a Syrian organization that works to support democratic transition in Syria, collaborated with lawyers and local communities to scan and safeguard over 2 million official documents. These documents include court records, property deeds and other legal documents. Property deeds constituted a third of the overall scanned documents. In a survey conducted by TDA with 10,000 IDPs, they found that only a third of forcibly displaced people were in possession of documents to prove their ownership. Similarly, the Norwegian Refugee Council (2016), conducted research on HLP systems but on a much smaller scale. In a survey of 362 refugee households in Lebanon and Jordan, they found that three-quarters of the participants possessed legally valid documents attesting to their HLP rights before the conflict. This shows that a quarter of the participants never held such documents even before the conflict. Furthermore, it was noted in the survey that only 20 per cent of the participants had the documentation in their possession after displacement. The findings of these two surveys raise critical questions about the future reconstruction of Syria and the complex realities of HLP ownership.

The Syrians who dared to dream of an alternative future, a future of freedom, justice and dignity, have found multiple wars against them. One of them is a war on their homes and the destruction of their built environment. Homes have been fought over and weaponized by those in power, erasing the presence of entire communities and targeting their HLP records to erase people from the pages of land and property documents that contained them.

The destruction of people's homes has been at the heart of the war in Syria as if these homes have been the frontline. The last decade has witnessed the wipe-out of entire neighbourhoods. This was the case of Masha' al-Arb'een neighbourhood in Hama (Figure Intro.1). In September 2012, government forces launched a massive offensive against this area with mortars and artillery prior to entering. After a few days of fighting, the opposition fighters in the neighbourhood retreated from the neighbourhood. Shortly after this, bulldozers directed by government forces entered the neighbourhood, demolishing thousands of buildings, according to residents. Human Rights Watch (HRW) conducted research on the deliberate destruction of homes in Syria, including this specific neighbourhood. In *Razed to the Ground: Syria's Unlawful Neighborhood Demolitions in 2012–2013* (HRW 2014), interviews were conducted with residents of Masha' al-Arb'een such as Umm Oday, who left her neighbourhood a month before the offensive for her safety. One day, she received a call from her neighbour informing her that her house was about to be demolished. When she returned, she found her street blocked by tanks and vehicles of the Syrian Army. She described the moment she lost her home (HRW 2014: 12):

FIGURE INTRO.1 Destruction of Masha' al-Arb'een, Hama, (*a*) 2008 and (*b*) 2019.
Source: Google Earth.

I yelled, screamed and cried for them to let me pass to see what is going on with my house. When they allowed me and other women to pass, the bulldozer was already demolishing houses while their owners stood outside watching. I begged the soldier to let me in to collect my belongings. He let me, but I had only a few minutes. After I left, the bulldozer demolished my house. Nothing was left of it, not even the walls.

Satellite images show that the first sign of demolition was on the morning of 28 September 2012. At the time, seventy heavy construction and utility vehicles were present in the neighbourhood and four armoured vehicles were visible which, according to HRW, supported the witnesses' claims that the fighting was over and the neighbourhood was under the government's control by the time of demolition. From 13 October 2012, satellite images showed the complete erasure of Masha' al-Arb'een, demolishing a built-up area of over 40 hectares. Government officials and pro-government media outlets claimed that the demolition of areas such as Masha' al-Arb'een, as well as other neighbourhoods in Damascus and Hama, were part of large-scale urban planning efforts that eradicated 'informal' and 'illegally constructed' buildings. At a time when millions of people were living under extreme conditions and had been pushed into poverty, the government found the time to erase what they labelled as 'informal' from cities and towns.

Since the start of the Syrian Revolution in March 2011, at least a third of the housing stock of the country has been destroyed. But it was not only homes that were destroyed. Cultural heritage sites have been wilfully targeted across different parts of the country such as the destruction in Palmyra by the Islamic State of Iraq and Syria (ISIS). Furthermore, everyday buildings and infrastructure projects have been bombed, including schools, local shops, markets, libraries, mosques, churches, hospitals and bridges. Paying attention to the destruction of architecture is essential in understanding violence in cities. As Rosie Bsheer (2020: 5) notes, 'erasure is not simply a countermeasure to the making of history: it is History'. By examining the erasure of the built environment, we can read *cities as archives*, Bsheer adds. Hence, we can read the story of wars through understanding the attempts to write and rewrite history, the cleansing of communities and the destruction of their documents, homes and, even in some cases, the graveyards of their family members.

Rewriting history is part of writing it. Through changing street names, removing revolutionary symbols, flags and graffiti, and building new memorials, statues and monuments, the 'winners' of wars narrate their own, one-sided version of history and bury the history of those opposing them. The Syrian government continues to rewrite history. In 2019, in a soap opera, they showed that bombing scenes and chemical attacks were prefabricated and staged. The scenes showed people mocking victims with Amal Arafa, a famous Syrian actress, playing a mother weeping over her child as if he was dead. The crew which was filming put on the head of the woman and her children white powder as if it was rubble from the ruins depicting scenes of chemical attacks. The scenes that turned the suffering of people into a scene in a comedy show have caused widespread outrage as it erases the pain of people. It led Arafa to write an apology for her role. This is only one attempt to rewrite history through public and popular outlets. Other tools have been used such as one of the most recent initiatives, Wathiqat Wattan (translates as a Homeland's Document), a 'non-governmental organization (NGO)', which is closely affiliated with and supported by the Syrian government. The NGO claims that it was launched to protect the contemporary national memory from loss, distortion or forgery, to protect the 'truth', the 'real history', as announced. In 2021, Wathiqat Wattan accepted submissions for a competition titled 'This is My Tale'. The NGO identifies its values on its website. One of them is the freedom of expression and accepting different opinions. This is not reflected in the work done by the NGO, which promotes and writes its own version of the history and 'truth' about the war in Syria with no mention of any opposition to the government except when described as 'armed groups' and 'terrorists'. So, not only has the tangible and material culture of people been destroyed, but even the writing of history is used as a tool to change the narrative in Syria.

War on the city

For over a decade now, the built environment in Iraq, Syria, Yemen and Libya (Figure Intro.2) has been radically transformed through the mass destruction of cities and villages and, before them, many cities throughout different times in history, such as Warsaw, Coventry, Hiroshima and Sarajevo, have been destroyed due to human conflicts and wars. The relationship between the built environment and violence, wars and conflicts has been widely researched. This increasingly growing body of research has focused on different lenses to theorize the geographical shifts of urban conflicts towards cities, their spatiality and their political causes and consequences (Graham 2009; Routledge 2010). The built environment within cities, towns and villages has become the site of battlefields and contestation as conflicts have moved beyond conventional armies (Kaldor and Sassen 2020).

In *Urbicide: The Politics of Urban Destruction*, Martin Coward (2009: 8) explains how architecture becomes the target for deliberate destruction at the time of conflict. Coward explains that the erasure of monumental and symbolic architecture should be understood and put in the context of a

FIGURE INTRO.2 Benghazi city centre, 2018.
Source: Nada Elfeituri.

'campaign of violence' against the built environment. For instance, the destruction of the Stari Most in Mostar should be seen as one case of a wider campaign against the built environment that characterized the 1992–5 Bosnian War. He notes that: 'whereas destruction of ancient bridges, museums and mosques can be understood as an assault upon the symbols of ethnic identity in Bosnia, the deliberate destruction of such mundane, profane buildings is more opaque. What is clear in such violence is that the buildings themselves were the target, and the violence was disproportionate to killing or displacing inhabitants.' Unlike Coward, several studies tend to focus on the destruction of monuments only whilst isolating them from the wider waves of violence.

Scholars writing about violence and conflicts have investigated not only how our built environments have been changed by conflicts (Grodach 2002; Larkin 2010; Bou Akar 2012; Riedlmayer 2016; Proudfoot 2017), but also how conflicts themselves have changed (Beall, Goodfellow and Rodgers 2013). As Saskia Sassin (2017) notes, nowadays, major cities are likely to be the frontline during wars, which is different from the two World Wars when large armies needed skies, oceans and fields to fight. This shift of conflicts towards everyday spaces has meant that an entire way of living has collapsed.

Residents find themselves at the heart of conflict (Piquard and Swenarton 2011). Tanks enter their neighbourhoods, snipers occupy their buildings and fighting groups knock down walls across homes to access the neighbourhood. In war on cities, soft targets such as bakery shops, schools and local markets are attacked, making everyday life a war in itself.

In contested cities, dividing lines emerge to control people's mobility and separate communities from one another. Public spaces become contested about who has the right to access them and who can protest in these spaces. Conflict infrastructures such as walls, fences, buffer zones, cement blocks and checkpoints emerge spatially within the built environment to segregate communities and create sectarian and homogenous geographies. With the emergence of these dividing frontiers, even infrastructure projects including main roads and train lines become sharp dividing edges between communities. As a result of these divisions, different ways of living emerge as if different cities are existing within the same city. Even spatially, the identity of space gets reshaped through architectural projects, flags, wall murals, graffiti and emblems, making these divided spaces canvases for rival narratives (Morrissey and Gaffikin 2006). Myths, fears and suspicions emerge across these divided communities, and trust gets tested, shaken and broken, whilst the social and physical mixing of these groups almost vanishes in harsh divided cities.

We have seen this occur in different divided cities in history, from the Berlin Wall to the Peace Wall in Belfast, from Beirut's Green Line to Nicosia's Green Line. Dividing the city is definitely not a new phenomenon (Marcuse 1993). History shows us not only the rise of these walls, but also their fall, such as the Berlin Wall, which divided the city between 1961 and 1989. However, even when walls fall, many non-physical divisions remain dividing people politically, socially and ideologically. During the last decade in Syria, communities have been divided on many different levels within the same city and also on the broader level across the country. In Homs, after the end of the multiple sieges, and the government's capture of the entire city, conflict infrastructure has been largely removed. Despite this, divisions remain sharp, and many people still refuse to visit certain parts of the city, fearing kidnap or hate crimes. Everyday life in Homs has been radically reshaped by the destruction of the built environment, but also by the inability of people in Homs to access public spaces that have become divided, contested and targeted. This includes, for instance, the New Clock Tower Square in Homs (I will explain this in more details in Chapter 1).

Much has been written about the deliberate destruction of the built environment at the time of conflict from different perspectives such as urban studies, architecture, heritage, human geography, international development and politics. Many of these studies, however, have benefitted from an understanding of the conflict through the lens of the built environment and the destruction of architecture. Despite the wide literature on conflicts and cities, however, there are still several challenges and limitations. I highlight some of them here.

First, urban studies 'as a discipline has been surprisingly slow to analyse how the experience of cities in the "South" might cause us to rethink urban knowledge and urban theory' (Mcfarlane 2010: 726). This also applies to the urban violence research that has been geographically limited. Mona Harb (2016) highlights the need to diversify the perspectives of urban studies on the city at war. She explains how current urban studies on conflicts and cities 'very much privilege cities of the global North, while cities at war elsewhere are less explored, even though they are increasingly the target of the US and Europe's defence strategies, as well as the testing grounds of many of the military and informational technologies implemented in policing and securing urban neighbourhoods'. These limitations are reflected by the lack of writing about cities that went through radical destruction in the aftermath of the Arab Spring in countries such as Libya, Yemen and Iraq. There is little scholarly work on what happened in these countries and how cities have been reshaped by long-term conflicts.

An example of this lack of knowledge is the destruction of Raqqa, a Syrian city that has become synonymous with ruins and urban misery. Between June and October 2017, the city was the site of mass bombardment by the Global Coalition led by the US (it included several forces, e.g. UK and France). With thousands of airstrikes within the four-month period (including 30,000 US artillery rounds), at least 1,600 civilians were killed and 80 per cent of the city has been reduced to rubble. The destruction included residential areas of people's homes, leaving tens of thousands of buildings uninhabitable. Little attention has been directed towards the Coalition's destruction of Raqqa. In 2019, Amnesty International launched a multimedia site to tell the story of the Coalition's destruction of Raqqa. I attended Amnesty International's exhibition and presentations at the Architectural Association (AA) in Bloomsbury in London. The exhibition focused on the struggle of civilians in Raqqa and the damage to their lives. Through videos, lectures, interactive maps and interviews with hundreds of people in Raqqa, the exhibition demonstrated the impact of conflict on the city and its people. The US-led Coalition to oust the Islamic State armed group from Raqqa claimed to have taken all the necessary measures to spare civilians and that it is the 'most precise' air campaign in the history of warfare. Amnesty International, however, shows how this rhetoric is a far cry from the reality (Allen 2019; Amnesty International 2019).

Raqqa is an example of a city that has been destroyed by foreign powers, but to date no academic research focuses on the city and its destruction. Other cities, including Gaza, Misrata, Deir ez-Zur, Mosul and Taiz remain underexplored despite all the losses each of these cities has endured. Other cities that were bombed and destroyed by foreign powers have been the focus of some academic research, such as the case of Belgrade which was bombed by the North Atlantic Treaty Organization (NATO) in 1999 (Badescu 2019).

This lack of studies on cities among the post-Arab Spring cities contrasts with the writings on urban violence in the aftermath of the September 11, 2001 attacks in cities such as Brussels, Paris and London (Coaffee 2004; Marcuse 2006; Jaffe 2017). The main question that should be asked is why do scholars on urban studies focus on certain contested areas and why do they avoid cities destroyed in the Arab region? Does this align with the 'First' and 'Third' World prejudice where some lives and cities are less valued than others?

Second, urban studies research on the destruction of the built environment at the time of wars and conflicts has been limited in its focus. It has become evident that in the wars of our times, cultural heritage sites and places that hold significant meaning to people have become contested, systematically targeted and wilfully destroyed (Smith et al. 2016; Brosché et al. 2017). Many of the emerging studies, however, tend to emphasize solely the destruction of the monumental and ancient architecture and celebrity-like cultural heritage sites. We have seen that in the case of the Mostar Bridge in 1993, Buddhas of Bamiyan in 2001, Timbuktu in 2012 and more recently Palmyra in 2015. The cinematic moments of destruction of significant cultural heritage sites have attracted global attention and outrage. In the past decade, there has been a proliferation of new centres and networks in response to the loss of heritage as if an entire 'industry' is emerging. For instance, in response to the increasing threats to archaeological sites, a programme was established in 2015 at the universities of Oxford, Leicester and Durham, called Endangered Archaeology in the Middle East and North Africa. At the Victoria and Albert Museum (V&A) in 2014, the Culture in Crisis programme was established. The landing page of the programme has an image of Palmyra. In the database portal, which was launched as part of the programme in 2019, there is a section for searching projects, with four suggested keywords: Syria is the first of them.

This attention to cultural heritage sites has led to endless numbers of studies, panel discussions, seminars, exhibitions, news articles and academic papers highlighting the destruction of these monuments, raising questions on the possible ways of preserving heritage at risk, and exploring ideas on how to remember, rehabilitate and reconstruct even if only digitally. At the United Nations Educational, Scientific and Cultural Organization (UNESCO), Irina Bokova (director-general of UNESCO, 2009–17) even proposed creating protected cultural heritage zones. As if stones are the focus, not the people, many scholars and cultural heritage 'experts' have dealt with Syria's heritage and its protection in separation and isolation of the Syrians. In *A Future in*

Ruins: UNESCO, World Heritage, and the Dream of Peace (2018), Lynn Meskell opens some of the uncomfortable and ethical questions that many academics working on heritage refuse to raise. She reflects on the proposals to create protected cultural heritage zones and notes that (2018: 182):

> The danger here is intervening in the rescue of purely material heritage, often a Classical antiquity for which Western nations consider themselves to be the legitimate inheritors, while not fully addressing those living and dying through the ongoing conflict or the resultant refugee crises. Western cultural elites have spent more time lamenting damage to a single site, the Classical ruins of Palmyra, than the destruction inflicted on hundreds of Islamic mosques and shrines across Iraq and Syria combined.

This interest in cultural heritage has also led to the neglect of the suffering, loss and trauma of impacted communities. In 'Heritage as War', Rosie Bsheer (2017: 729) notes that the brutal destruction of material history by ISIS provoked a global public attention. However:

> Most media outlets and preservationist agencies have covered and condemned such destruction much more so than they did the pain, suffering and death that the United States, local governments, and other actors inflicted upon human beings in either country. Such inconsistencies in reporting and advocacy ultimately frame the destruction of material history as more tragic and reprehensible than the loss of (presumably Muslim) life. (Bsheer 2017: 729)

Many of the emerging studies on Syria's built environment have failed to examine the impact of the destruction of everyday spaces and places. This interest in monumental and ancient cultural heritage sites has overshadowed the mass destruction of everyday, mundane and lesser-known architecture such as homes, schools, local shops, bridges and roads. These are the spaces that many people in Syria would relate to and experience in their everyday life. The destruction of the home in Syria is not limited to the destruction of people's physical home, but also to the disorientation they endure due to the destruction of their sense of identity and belonging.

Third, very often, research on cities and conflicts, displacement and refugees, suffers from the lack of engagement with the impacted communities or understanding their loss and struggle. From the comfort of cities such as London, Berlin, Cambridge and New York, many academics who come from privileged backgrounds and belong to prestigious institutions have relied only on online reports to write about the conflict in Syria rather than talking to the people whose lives have been reshaped by wars. So distant and alienated are these academics from the struggle of the suffering communities that the voices, stories, narratives and experiences of the impacted people get hidden in these studies, marginalized and silenced. Suddenly, you feel that the human struggle has been removed from these studies, that we are talking about stones not human lives.

Some academics publish about Syria without any data collection from the impacted communities, whilst others hire assistants to do so. Principle investigators (PIs) who might not know the language, culture or context of Syria might rely on 'research assistants' to conduct research in countries like Türkiye, Jordan or Lebanon, where millions of Syrians have found refuge since 2011. But very rarely do these PIs, who succeed in having giant research grants, visit their 'research field' or connect with the impacted communities. In some cases, they would visit for a few days or weeks. Yet, they would present and publish the work themselves whilst they silence, exclude and marginalize the work of their 'assistants' who might be conducting and writing most of the work in the studied region. I remember once a white British academic who had never done any work on Syria, nor knew the language of the country or its political situation, telling me that he was going to 'Oman' in Jordan to visit a 'large' refugee camp. He was unable to remember its name. He did not know that Amman is the capital of Jordan, that Oman is a different country, nor was he able to recall the name of the Zaatari refugee camp which he was supposed to visit as part of the multi-hundred-thousand pound research grant he and his colleagues got. Mayssoun Sukarieh and Stuart Tannock (2018: 7) have written about the emergence of the Syrian refugee research 'industry' in the UK. In 'Subcontracting Academia: Alienation, Exploitation and Disillusionment in the UK Overseas Syrian Refugee Research Industry', they explain how some of the funded research projects are 'alien to (or estranged from) the immediate concerns of Syrian refugees and other local communities in Lebanon' (2018: P7). They add that:

> The overseas Syrian refugee research industry has become a significant business operation for many UK universities and academics: it is not just regional experts who are applying for research funding, but others with no previous experience of Syria or Lebanon, and little to no ability to speak, understand or read Arabic. (2018: P5)

Very often projects are designed in countries, for example, in the UK and the US, without any engagement with impacted Syrian communities and are imposed on fragile and vulnerable communities that are struggling with their everyday lives. The scope of these projects might be seen as offensive to Syrians who are dealing with their everyday trauma, whilst seeing their own pain and struggle turned into a funding project of academics and opportunists.

For these academics, Syrians might be the last they would engage with, but they see in their work on Syria an opportunity to get fundable projects important for their academic career. This is why I wrote a paper titled, 'Our Pain, Their Heritage Project' (2022).

In the paper, I argued that these projects are celebrated and talked about in the UK as a success and framed as notable projects. But they often fail to bring the voices of Syrians to the conversation. These projects as well as many other presentations and panel discussions are often presented by Syria 'experts'. It felt many times like our pain, our struggle, our narrative had been stolen from us. It feels like we have become the funding opportunity for others, but these others simply do not see us. No wonder so many of my Syrian friends and colleagues refuse to speak to those academics who come with a predetermined set of questions and research projects that lack the understanding of our struggle and pain. They presented our story without giving the space for Syrians to narrate their own story. The voices of impacted communities who live with the aftermath of destruction and the loss of homes that we have endured in Syria have been excluded in many of the Syria projects and debates. This is also the case with many discussions surrounding the future reconstruction of Syria, that will be seen by many individuals, governments and companies as an economic opportunity that attracts international architects, politicians, policymakers and academics.

Saying that, Syrian voices have pushed the boundaries to tell the story of Syria and its people. Since 2011, architects, academics, activists and urban planners have created a new body of work that focuses on different themes related to the impact of war on the built environment and local communities. This includes the work of architects based inside Syria, such as the publications of Marwa Al-Sabouni whose work has been widely shared, placing her city, Homs, on international stages. Her writing has appeared in many news publications, including the BBC, the *Guardian* and the *Financial Times*. Emad Al Masri, an academic also based in Syria, has published several articles on Homs. Outside Syria, architects in different countries and from different parts of Syria have contributed to the post-2011 architectural discourse, such as the work of Houda Jwadi, Sawsan Abou Zainedin, Hani Fakhani and Wesam Al Asali.

Many of the Syrians inside and outside the country, within the professions of architecture, hope to work more on the questions of destruction and reconstruction. However, this is challenging with the lack of working opportunities and access to publishers and grants. Inside Syria, with the collapse of the economy, several architects have been pushed to flee the country whilst others had to change their careers as an act of survival. Some of those outside Syria have been able to find working opportunities on Syria, but this has been only a small number of individuals who either work in academic institutions or charities. This is all, however, shaped by access to funds and institutions to undertake the work. Therefore, many Syrian architects, inside and outside the country, have ended up working in a personal capacity when no financial support was available.

Domicide: The destruction of home

Whilst a growing body of work has emerged in the past decade on the relationship between the built environment and violence in Syria, little attention has been focused on the consequences of destruction on impacted communities. In *Life and Words: Violence and the Descent into the Ordinary,* Veena Das (2006: 8) writes that her main interest in her book is not in describing 'the moments of horror, but rather in describing what happens to the subject and the world when the memory of such events is folded into ongoing relationships'. I am similar to Das in being interested in the aftermath of destruction, in the violence that takes place in everyday urban life and in the impact of this violence on communities whose lives have been reshaped by the horrors of war.

I therefore ask: What does it mean to lose one's home? What does it mean to be uprooted from one's home and from the people you love and cherish? What does it mean to lose something every day? To lose the familiar streets, buildings and squares, to lose your city? Even when you lose them, slowly and gradually, what does it mean to walk on the path of life knowing that even the return to the ruins of your city, the chance to say a final goodbye to the ones you lost, the visit to your erased home, is impossible?

In this book, I build on domicide as a concept which J. Douglas Porteous and Sandra E. Smith (2001: 19) define as the: 'planned, deliberate destruction of home causing suffering to the dwellers'. This destruction tends to reinforce existing socio-spatial struggles of segregation, inequality and oppressions forced upon people who have already been penalized, disadvantaged and excluded (Zhang 2018). Porteous and Smith elaborate that domicide might result in:

> the destruction of a place of attachment and refuge; loss of security and ownership; restrictions on freedom; partial loss of identity; and a radical decentring from place, family, and community. There may be a loss of historical connection; a weakening of roots; and partial erasure of the sources of memory, dreams, nostalgia, and ideas. (2001: 63)

Domicide first appeared as a neologism in 1988 in articles and speeches by Porteous as standing between 'domesticity' and 'domicile'. Domicide puts 'home' as a central concept (Latin: *domus*), and the deliberate destruction of this home through its suffix, 'cide'. The suffix 'cide' refers not to the death or decline, but rather to the deliberate killing, as in suicide or urbicide, the deliberate destruction of the urban (Campbell, Graham and Monk 2007; Ramadan 2009). As Bob Catterall (2014: 385), the founder of *City Journal*, notes, domicide is the 'murder of homes and ways of life, though permitted by ruling ideologies, law and associated contained consciences'.

The intentional destruction of home is thus selective, causing deep suffering to individuals and communities. Yunpeng Zhang who writes about the social suffering and symbolic violence in China notes that what victims of domicide have in common is their unaccountability in social and numeric senses (2018). Some bodies or bodily experiences are seen as irrelevant, and in some cases, land has even become more valuable than the people who live on it. Constructing unaccountability takes on several disguises according to Zhang. At best, a paternalistic view is constructed projecting victims of domicide as inferior and that domicide is in their own interest. As a result, domicidal projects are based on the normalization of victims of domicide, portraying their suffering as a sacrifice for the collective greater good. In the worst case, however, the 'othering' processes within communities constructs an image that dehumanizes the victims of domicide or even considers them as enemies of the state who need to be defeated, displaced, punished or killed (Porteous and Smith 2001). This is the case in Syria where some bodies or bodily experiences are seen as irrelevant and are completely removed from their homes and land. The destruction of their homes has been justified and covered in the name of 'War on Terror' at the time of 'war', or even in the name of 'modernization', 'development' or even 'reconstruction' at the time of 'peace'. The study of domicide inevitably invites us to get closer to the human struggle when people's places are razed to the ground. As Porteous and Smith (2001: 6) note, 'place is meaningful to people, and the place called home is the most meaningful of all. When it is threatened, we are roused to defend it.' Once this place is threatened, we have a disorientating experience as if we are out of place. We also learn in domicide that:

> home is not simply one's dwelling but can also be one's homeland or native region. It is one of the obvious facts of life, so often overlooked, that people are not merely attached to other people but also to familiar objects, structures, and environments that nurture the self, support the continuity of life, and act as props to memory and identity. (Porteous and Smith 2001: 6)

Central to the concept of domicide is 'home'. In their book, *Home*, Alison Blunt and Robyn Dowling (2006) note that home is a significant geographical and social concept. It is not only a shelter, a three-dimensional structure, but also a matrix of social relations with a wide range of symbolic and ideological meanings. Blunt and Dowling argue that home is both a space and a concept which can exist on different scales, such as the body, the house, the city or the nation. In their book, they propose the term 'critical geographies of home', which includes three cutting components: home as simultaneously material and imaginative, the nexus between home, power and identity, and home as multi-scalar.

First, home as material and imaginative means that it is not only the physicality or even geography where people reside, but also the imagined home. In this way, home can be another country or place where people have metaphorical attachment and a sense of belonging. Second, the nexus between home, power and identity refers to different experiences people have with home based on, for instance, age, ethnicity, gender, sexuality and political opinions and affiliations. Experiences vary and home, which has often been referred to as the site of security, safety, belonging and tranquillity, can be seen as the site of domestic violence, fear, abuse and insecurity (Akesson, Basso and Denov 2016), such as the experiences of many women around the world who face violence at home. However, 'negative experiences, such as gender violence or patriarchal oppression, do not contradict the ideal of home as a place of sanctuary, fundamental to the formation of identity and the basic needs for security and control' (Zhang 2018: 192). Third, home as multi-scalar emphasizes the personal relations to public and political worlds. Accordingly, the 'feelings of home' can be stretched across the world, with connections to a nation, a house or imagined spaces of home, which are all central to people's identities. In this sense, home can be conceived on different scales, from a small room to a neighbourhood to one's supportive environment to a city or even larger territorial unit.

The study of violence, movement and forced displacement in relationship with losing homes and then recreating them has already been an important theme in anthropology and refugee studies. An example of this is the work of Stef Jansen and Staffan Löfving. In their co-edited book, *Struggles for Home: Violence, Hope and the Movement of People*, Jansen and Löfving (2009) bring together ethnographic case studies from different countries, including Palestine, Southern Spain, Sri Lanka and Guatemala. In these cases, the book focuses not only on the movement of people away from violence searching for places to remake home, but also the struggles for it. These struggles for home are investigated through the contestation of emplacement, the analysis of memories, geographical belongings and the practices of attachment and detachment from place. For the editors, home is attached and detached from places 'through relations of power that attribute certain qualities to them, such as security, familiarity, wealth or freedom'.

Similar to their work, I bring conflict studies in closer dialogue with the notions of home (Porteous and Smith 2001; Tuathail and Dahlman 2006;

Zhang 2018). I trace the concept of home, and its destruction, domicide, through different scales, sites, geographies and temporalities. By doing so, I look at domicide not solely through the lens of losing an individual home, but I also expand it to think about the collective loss of a sense of home when neighbourhoods are razed to the ground, when the sense of belonging is broken and when an entire way of living has collapsed. By Home, I refer not only to the tangible loss of the material structures and infrastructure, but I also move beyond it to explore themes of memory, identity, belonging and exile.

I argue that domicide is not only performed at the time of war and conflict, but also at the time of 'peace' and in the name of reconstruction. Before 2011, much of the identity of Syrian cities was changed under the cover of urbanization. This led to the demolition of old traditional homes and palaces to lay the foundations for new buildings and infrastructure projects. As in other contested and ruined cities, in Syrian cities today, reconstruction is not about rebuilding the tangible built environment – that can be used as a powerful propaganda tool by those in political and economic power – but about building a place for all people; a place for everyone, for the marginalized, the poor, the disadvantaged and the refugees, not a place of exclusion that benefits the few rich elites at the expense of the wider population. However, many of the debates on future reconstruction bring with them new waves of domicidal projects that would erase what remains in Syria and push the marginalized into further marginalization (this will be explored in detail in Chapter 5).

Several scholars have used the concept of domicide as a framework to link the social suffering of people to their destroyed structures. Zhang is one of these scholars who have written eloquently and profoundly about domicide and property dispossession (2015, 2017a, 2017b). In his work, Zhang brings out the lived experiences of the unmaking and remaking of a home for those who were displaced in Shanghai. He focuses in one of his publications on the displacement of people whose homes where demolished in order to build World Expo 2010 (2018: 203). One of the powerful and critical points in Zhang's work is his methodological approach that brings to the heart of the conversation people's voices, stories and narratives. These bodily experiences of home as the space of refuge, comfort, security, rootedness and belonging bring the research of conflict and violence very carefully and very closely to the impacted communities, to their losses and trauma. These stories bring to life the losses of people, when these stories are often lost, forgotten and unheard as if people are the last to care about in these projects. Here is the voice of one of the people Zhang interviewed. It is a lament to the loss of home and the grief for not having a memory of it:

> It was so deep in your mind, you know? Decades of life there . . . All had gone. It was empty. I stood there with feelings that I could hardly describe.

> My heart was empty. All empty. There was no way back, no way back. I should have taken some pictures. Back then, I did not realise I need pictures. Now, it is all in my memory all in my memory. (Zhang 2018: 203, interview of May 2012)

I have been moved by Zhang's work and its ability to bring the voices of impacted people closer to the readers. In these voices, I have connected with the struggle of the people and found similarities in the struggle of Syrians whose homes have been wilfully destroyed, though of course in a totally different context and situation. In the lament of home, I have often heard people mentioning pictures of their lost beloved home, and the sadness of not only losing home, but even the pictures of it. When I spoke with Omama Zankawan, a London-based Syrian from Homs, she told me:

> We simply don't have any photo of our house before it was burnt and destroyed. My mother was trying to find a small piece of our home. But she couldn't. The only memory I have from my home is in my mind. (London, 2019)

Zankawan's quote is similar to the person interviewed by Zhang; two extremely different places and contexts, but both people struggling to capture the image of a lost home, and wishing they had a reimagination of their lost home, longing for a time and place they can no longer reclaim, even in photos.

Extreme and everyday domicide

Domicide and the widespread destruction of both the symbolic and the physical home have been taking place across different parts of the world and through different times of history. Domicide, however, is not only limited to the time of war and conflict, but also occurs in times of 'peace'. This is exactly what Porteous and Smith (2001) present in their book, *Domicide: The Global Destruction of Home*, as they put domicide in two categories: 'extreme domicide' (generally abnormal, massive and infrequent) and 'everyday domicide' (frequent and smaller scale).

I bring up this notion of domicide in war and peace as I focus in this book on the interconnection between everyday and extreme domicide. Whilst many would imagine or assume that destruction is only limited to the time of war, I explore in this book the relationship between everyday and extreme domicide. Everyday domicide has shaped cities and villages in Syria from before 2011, as waves of destruction radically reshaped the urban fabric and destroyed cultural heritage sites. This everyday domicide might again cause further damage to local communities in the name of reconstruction. Historically, we have seen how reconstruction can result in more destruction to cities and damage to communities (Nagel 2002; Hubbard, Faire and Lilley 2003; Wollentz 2017). These fears and concerns about new destructions yet to come are present today in the emerging conversations on the future reconstruction of Syria (Said and Yazigi 2018; DiNapoli 2019). I expand the knowledge on the interconnection of everyday and extreme domicide, between peace and war domicide. I, therefore, not only look at the wartime domicide that the world has witnessed in the past decade, but introduce the concept of slow violence that for decades has been causing displacement, destruction and loss to the built environment. I also link pre-war and wartime domicide with reconstruction plans that bring with them a future in ruins.

By doing so, I also contribute to the increasingly growing literature that focuses on the weaponization of architecture and urban planning and the destruction of cities both in war and peace (Fawaz, Harb and Gharbieh 2012; Unruh 2016; Imady 2019). By engaging with the literature on the links between peace and war, I show how architecture and urban planning can also be used to fight during 'peace' as tools and strategies that continue the damage of wartime.

Wartime domicide

In times of war and conflict, people's homes and their cultural heritage are destroyed not only for 'military purposes' or in the name of 'war on terror', but rather are also demolished, bulldozed and bombed wilfully. Scholars and activists have shown how the built environment has been weaponized in Syria. The destruction of people's homes has been seen as a tool for punishment, displacement and violence against those who oppose the regime or sympathize with the uprising. The levelling of people's homes did not only mean the eradication of physical buildings and structures, but also meant the eradication of the conditions of possibility and existence for their personal identities. Through domicide, people have been either killed or forcibly displaced away from the areas in which they lived. Their entire way of life has collapsed, causing more suffering to people who have already been marginalized. This happened in many towns and cities in Syria where the government erased 'informal' areas at the time of conflict. Even now, after years of destruction as in Hama, these ruined neighbourhoods have been kept without any development. Destruction of the built environment in Syria is by no means exceptional as this has been the case in many cities throughout history.

'Peacetime' domicide

In 'peace' times, domicidal plans can be the product of political, bureaucratic and corporate projects. People's homes and their cultural heritage sites are wilfully destroyed in the name of modernization, development, regeneration, urban renewals and rebirth to enable the emergence of new buildings and infrastructure projects such as roads, airports, luxury hotels, skyscrapers and national parks (Bou Akar 2019; De Cesari and Dimova 2019). In other situations, 'informal' and 'unauthorized' areas are demolished, causing suffering to their inhabitants. For instance, in China, tower blocks emerge after demolishing people's homes and evicting them. The 'destructive construction', as Kaixun Sha (2014: 391) puts it, 'violates the value of people first. It inevitably leads to ruthless deprivation, uprooted lives, eradication of history in cities, land-less farmers and an endless petition process by the dispossessed who seek justice.'

Governments propose utopian urban scenarios for imagined cities. In this process, the urban poor are evicted from their homes against their will. Their homes are demolished to lay the foundations for megaprojects that deliberately ignore the suffering of those expelled from the places in which they lived. Omnia Khalil has written prolifically about the damages and destruction that took place in Cairo, Egypt, during the past decade. She explains in her research how people's homes, shops, markets and souks have been destroyed gradually in the quest of building a 'surreal' Cairo that replaces the people who lived in certain areas with other people. In 2008, government policies in Egypt started to map cities based on safe and unsafe settlements defining the built environment as planned and unplanned. Khalil explains how the government discourses labelled places of the urban poor as *Ashwa'yaat*, which means 'chaotic neighbourhood' (Khalil 2015). These discourses began to criminalize the urban poor who live in the so-called slums. However, violence against them manifested itself in the name of redevelopment, pushing the poor into harsher, more extreme, more vulnerable living conditions (Khalil 2021). Both in China and Egypt, domicide is used to erase people's way of life, destroying their sense of community and their sense of belonging.

The 'War on Terror' and the 'war on terrorists' have also been used as false rhetoric to justify domicide. In Saudi Arabia, the 400-year-old Mousawarah neighbourhood (which means the 'Walled' in Arabic), in Al Awamiyah, saw layers of history, memory and meaning bulldozed completely to the ground (HRW 2017). The entire neighbourhood was targeted and then razed to the ground, demolishing hundreds of properties in the name of development (Figure Intro.3). Not only were people expelled from their beloved homes, but their ownership was given to the government. Satellite images show the complete desolation of the neighbourhood in 2017. Following the radical

FIGURE INTRO.3 Mousawarah, (*a*) 2015, (*b*) 2017 and (*c*) 2019.
Source: Google Earth.

erasure of the neighbourhood, a newly built site emerged replacing hundreds of homes that were demolished with a very small number of 'cultural' buildings. Karima Bennoune, the United Nations (UN) Special Rapporteur in the field of cultural rights, notes that:

> Historic buildings have been irremediably burned down and damaged by the use of various weapons by the military, forcing residents out of their homes and of the neighbourhood, fleeing for their lives. (UN Human Rights 2017)

On several popular media platforms, the Saudi authorities show the project as a new cultural site that is rooted in the heritage of the local population. On such media platforms, the project is described as a 'victory for development over terror' (MBC News 2019), whilst projecting the old neighbourhood as 'uninhabitable', 'old', 'informal area' and 'harmful' to the local people (MBC News 2019; Al Arabiya 2019). The Saudi authorities considered this historic quarter of largely Shia Muslims to be a breeding ground for opposition groups and anti-government protests. Little is shown on these media platforms of what the people of the neighbourhood feel during and after the destruction. A US-based Awamiya native and activist, Mohammed Al Zaher, said in an interview that 'people didn't want to leave their places. The truth is, nobody wanted to leave their home . . . they were happy' (Qiblawi 2017). UK-based Ameen al-Nimr, who left the town of Al Awamiyah in late 2011, described the operation as a 'collective punishment' (The New Arab and agencies 2017). There is a lack of online materials that document the voices of displaced communities. One exception is a video showing women walking in their narrow alleyways of Mousawarah, calling for help to save their homes from demolition. One of the women said: 'whatever happens to us, we are not leaving our homes. This is our cemetery. They want us to leave our home by force.' Another woman said: 'these are our homes that raised us and raised our children. This is our land and this is our cemetery and these are our homes. Our graves are here, we will never leave. If they want to come and bury us in it, then let them come and bury us in it. We will never leave, let them kill us here.' Yet another woman said: 'those who want to help the oppressed, stop our evacuation, stop the decision to evacuate us from our homes. We don't want money. We don't want [other] homes. We want a home where Allah protects us. We want the inheritance of our ancestors and our fathers. We want to live in it and die in it.'

Writing Syria from afar

The main focus in this book is the city of Homs, which has been radically reshaped since 2011, a city where more than three-quarters of its neighbourhoods have been damaged either partially or heavily. Whilst some chapters are rooted in Homs, I engage with the wider conversations surrounding the built environment in different parts of Syria, as in the case of Damascus. Through the transformation of cities, its everyday urban life during the war, domicide, the destruction of memory, the changing demographics of people and the levelling of people's architectures, the book brings together questions about homesickness and the strangeness of people 'exiled' in their own city. I explore pressing contemporary issues of conflict studies, such as memory, loss of the familiar, displacement, nostalgia for the old days and the destruction of both monumental and everyday buildings. In addition, I explain some of the local responses to destruction and displacement, and the struggle of architects, academics and urban planners to bring the scattered pieces of their country together through reimagining their role at a time of war; rehabilitating the damaged built environment and debating the future reconstruction of Syria.

The objective of this book is to bring the lived experiences of the making and unmaking of home to the centre of struggles at the time of war. I build on domicide, the killing of home, which I arrived at because of the readings that I have been doing of the wide literature of urban conflict studies (Pullan 2011; Ragab 2011; Bou Akar 2012; Fawaz 2017; Isakhan and Meskell 2019). Scholars who contributed to studies on cities and conflicts have highlighted how the built environment has been targeted wilfully at the time of violence (Bevan 2006; Coward 2009; Fregonese 2009; Abujidi 2014). A very small part of this literature has picked up the concept of domicide, which I hope to contribute towards. In domicide I have found a linkage between the built environment and the emotional attachment people have to the spaces and places they live in. Domicide also brings people's grief, struggle and loss to the fore when compared to many writings on conflict studies that separate the built environment from its people and fail to engage with the voices of impacted communities.

Whilst conducting my research from my exile, I relied on interviews with Syrian residents and with members of the Syrian diaspora. By engaging with Syrians and narrating their stories at the time of war, this research brings the human agency element to the questions of domicide and reconstruction in Syria; a dimension that is often lost in studies on the Syrian crisis and even more broadly in the research field of cities at war. Interviews were conducted both with professionals working in the built environment field (such as academics, architects, civil engineers and university students) and with impacted people who feel that they are the last to be consulted in shaping the future of their built environment. Very often, the voices of impacted people are missing in the emerging debates on Syria's built environment. This is why I have chosen not only to speak with architects, in the hope of bridging the gap that has been widening between people and architects. This gap, however, has not only been seen during the past decade, but also for years before 2011. Before the war, there were no meaningful programmes for community engagement in urban planning or participatory architecture, and hence, local communities have often felt that they are unheard and neglected in determining the fate of their own built environment.

Even fewer interviews have been undertaken with academics, artists and researchers working on conflict studies on Syria or other contested geographies and across different periods of history (such as Warsaw and Coventry after the Second World War, Beirut after the Civil War and Berlin after the fall of the Berlin Wall). In these interviews, old questions become relevant today: how to rebuild devastated cities? What powers shape reconstruction? How to remember the time of war through the preservation of ruins? And what consequences have these reconstructions brought to communities after decades of rebuilding? Many other questions have emerged that I found similar to the questions Syrian architects and urban planners are thinking about today. In 2020, I released a project with three short films on domicide. The films brought the work of some of these academics and impacted communities into the conversation of destruction and memory.

Over the course of more than four years, I have spoken with people who brought me close to the human struggle. I have found in interviews a way to understand the conflict from the bottom up, from the people on the ground narrating how their everyday living conditions have been transformed by conflict and challenged on many fronts. I have found in this anthropological approach to the urban, a way to get to the individual story and to resist the disappearance of these struggles from the studies of conflicts and cities. Through these interviews with people from different sects and different neighbourhoods in Homs, I was able to capture multiple perspectives from within. As Homs remains divided on so many different levels, and as many of the people do not talk to one another, I found myself in several cases aware of projects, initiatives and charities in the city that some of my interviewees there were unaware of. Fear and the lack of trust still divides people. Our conversations have been limited, with all the fear people have to talk about the situation around them. My positionality, as someone from Homs, who grew up and studied in the city, has enabled me to connect and be connected with people who know me or know someone who knows me. This has been crucial to get access to people. Without these links, I would be disconnected from the country from which I have been displaced for over a decade.

Beyond open and sometimes semi-structured interviews, I constantly engaged informally with Syrians who reside in Syria (through online conversations) and with the Syrian diaspora so as to have an in-depth understanding of the impact of war on their everyday life, their memory before and during the years of war. My connection with Homs has been constant through phone or video calls and messages, so, although I was not there, my connection has been permanent, and very often painful as living conditions continue to worsen. This is, of course, a research limitation as I have been unable to visit Syria, and many would argue, who am I to speak about a country from my exile? However, I lived in the city for twenty-three years and, through my interviews, I brought some of the voices of people who remain in the city to the heart of this work.

I have been in touch with people who lost their homes and family members. I spoke with people whose lives have turned into a practice of waiting, mastering loss every single day. Through their mobile phones, they took me online to their homes. It was painful to hear and see that people are struggling to get their basic needs, their weekly bread, electricity, hot water or heating system on the coldest days. I often felt the inadequacy of language to capture the enormity of human experiences. Sometimes words failed me to put these struggles on paper and listening to people talking about their damaged lives has been damaging. I bring this struggle of people to the heart of domicide so that it is not forgotten. Therefore, whenever I quote a text from any of these interviews, I pay attention to avoid objectification of the voices in order not to present difficult experiences in a simplified and shallow way that aestheticizes and romanticizes people's suffering, but rather to reflect on them in a situated, sensitive and respectable manner. I apologize if I failed to do justice to these stories. This pain is also mine, and this struggle is also my own.

I reviewed the emerging literature on Syria's built environment (Rabbat 2016; Imady 2019; Qaddour 2020; *The Syria Report* 2020). This includes academic writings (Mooney 2014; Vignal 2014; Proudfoot 2017; Chatty 2018; Al Asali 2020; Mazur 2020), newspapers articles (BBC 2011; Doucet 2013; Fox 2017) and reports published by international organizations such as the UN and World Bank (UNESCO n.d.; UNHCR 2017; World Bank 2019). The work of Amnesty International and Human Rights Watch has been of great relevance, as both of them have published several articles, not only on the weaponization of the built environment but also on its impact on communities (HRW 2011, 2018, 2019; Amnesty International 2015). Other resources comprise filmed materials, drawings, maps, speeches, reconstruction plans and visions. The research I did for these materials has always been in both Arabic and English.

Visual materials have been analysed including videos released on new proposed projects for reconstruction, architectural drawings and plans. These materials have often been found in newspapers (local and international) reporting the crises in Syria rather than in academic articles. I have also studied the webpages of the city councils, local and international charities and ministries. Social media has been the only way to get the most recent updates – often scattered – as many local charities in Syria do not use online websites and rely solely on social media as the medium to communicate. Concerns that I raised about the sensitivity of the interviews are also similar to the use of images. I believe that images are important to the understanding of a particular urban situation, but there is a need to be careful not to aestheticize and glorify violence and destruction through such images. Rather, images should be used in a thoughtful and sensitive manner.

I have kept a high level of engagement with colleagues and friends working on related themes to domicide. This includes attending, participating or presenting at seminars, webinars, workshops, lectures, festivals and focus groups. Through these events, I have developed new connections and enjoyed belonging to different networks and meeting new people. I have also been able to learn about the individual and collective work that has been done across the world in response to the destruction of the built environment in Syria. These participations were crucial to understanding the different perspectives and approaches towards destruction and reconstruction and the wide range of people who are shaping the narrative.

The argument

This book offers an analysis of the crises in Syria with a main focus on Homs, the third largest city in the country. I keep the concepts of home as a central focus to think about destruction and reconstruction and to understand the impact of domicide on internally displaced residents and on Syrians abroad. Through the lens of domicide, I aim to move beyond the destruction of monumental sites to go deeply into the physical and social trauma of destruction and displacement from home. Attention is directed towards rebuilding lives, home and shelter, both inside and outside Syria, which will further widen the understanding of what happens to people forced out of their homes by conflict. A reflection on the ways Syrians cope with their everyday life during the conflict will add further understanding of the crisis which is often studied from the perspective of refugees rather than from the point of view of those who stay and support their cities in times of war.

The book consists of five chapters. Chapter 1 gives a brief presentation about the city of Homs before and after the start of the war in 2011. By looking at Homs before and during the conflict, the chapter shows how the city witnessed different waves of slow violence before the war, which accumulated in faster, more radical and intense forms of destruction since 2011. Furthermore, I will discuss the impact of conflict on the city and the people. To do so, I explore domicide on different scales and in different spaces and places, ranging from a loss of a single house to a wider loss of public spaces. With the mass destruction of Homs and the killing and displacement of its people, I show how many residents have a disorientating experience in their own city, with a sense of loss and exile even for those who have stayed in their own homes.

In Chapter 2, I will look at the local responses to destruction and displacement inside Homs, and the role of local and international charities and organizations that function from within Syria, in helping communities in their search for home. This chapter will investigate the strategies, mechanisms and patterns that were followed by some of the local charities in Homs despite the extreme conditions they were facing. I also show how, with the struggle of local and international organizations to respond to the scale of destruction, internally displaced people are becoming 'architects' in their quest to access shelter. Today, years after the end of fighting in Homs, there are no reconstruction projects yet, but rather, rehabilitation projects of partially damaged buildings. I will also turn to the public space again to show how it has become further contested after the end of the fighting with the emergence of new one-sided memorials that divide people instead of bringing them back together.

Having outlined the concept of domicide, the destruction of home in Homs and the responses to destruction inside Syria, Chapter 3 will turn to outside of Syria. I will explore imagined homelands in exile, for those who are unable to return to Syria. I visit the cafes and restaurants that opened outside Syria and join the protests, memorials and sit-ins organized by Syrians outside their country. From their exiles, the Syrian diaspora attempt to build a new home as they reimagine and reconstruct a Syria through different cultural and social events. As part of this chapter, I will also focus on the work of artists who are not from Syria but who have responded to domicide in Syria.

Chapter 4 will deal with the emerging debates on the reconstruction of Syria, their motivations and dynamics. First, it will focus on the reconstruction plans, decrees, projects and conversations happening inside Syria and across different cities. It will show how the reconstruction of sites is selective, and how it is used as propaganda by those in power, without engaging with locals who have been impacted by the conflict. Second, it will look at the emerging debates on reconstruction outside Syria by Syrians and those from around the world working in different geographies and on different projects in relation to Syria's culture, heritage, architecture and reconstruction. The chapter will also identify a number of the fears that some of these debates bring with them, such as silencing communities and not enabling them to grieve, erasing the memory of certain groups and whitewashing ownership of owners who have fled the country. Chapter 5 will present concluding remarks and suggest some ideas for resisting domicide.

1

Domicide

Slow violence, division and destruction

In the Introduction, I argued that the violence of domicide is not only limited to times of war, but also occurs in times of 'peace'. In this chapter, I explore this interlink between war and peace with a focus on Homs, the third largest city in Syria, and a city that has come to be known as the Capital of the Revolution. I build on the work of Rob Nixon, the author of *Slow Violence and the Environmentalism of the Poor*, who argues that we need to move beyond the one-off image of destruction 'to engage a different kind of violence, a violence that is neither spectacular nor instantaneous, but rather incremental and accretive, its calamitous repercussions playing out across a range of temporal scales' (2011: 2). This is what Nixon refers to as 'slow violence' that is 'out of sight, a violence of delayed destruction that is dispersed across time and space, an attritional violence that is typically not viewed as violence at all'. Through the lens of slow violence, I revisit the struggles in Homs before 2011. I, therefore, look at different sites and events that perhaps have not been viewed as violence at all at the time, but rather, as architectural and urban planning projects to build a 'better' Homs. By observing these struggles before 2011, I also attempt to link them to the wider questions of destruction and reconstruction that connect what happened before 2011 with the destruction that took place after 2011. In his book, Nixon asks, 'how can we turn the long emergencies of slow violence into stories dramatic enough to rouse public sentiment and warrant formal intervention, these emergencies whose repercussions have given rise to some of the most critical challenges of our time?' (2011: 3). In this chapter, I engage with these questions in the context of Homs and visit spaces of identity, inequality, protests and war.

Space of identity

Homs is known as the City of the Black Stones for the use of the black basalt stones in its old and contemporary built environments. These stones were used in a wide range of places and spaces that formed the architectural identity of the city, including public squares, monuments, houses, souks, hammams, mosques, churches and administrative and leisure buildings. Very often, alternating rows of black and white stones have been used in what is known as the ablaq architectural style, making it unmistakably a recognizable image of the city. The use of these stones has become part of the architectural imagination for Homsis and could be seen prominently in the Old City, and in more moderate amounts beyond it. Even when these stones were unavailable or unaffordable, some people would paint their interior walls or exterior facades in black and white to replicate this style.

Homs had multiple nicknames. In addition to the City of the Black Stones, it was also known as the City of Khalid ibn al-Walid, a Muslim commander who was born in Mecca and died in Homs. Multiple places and spaces have been named after him, spatially cementing his name into the city. This includes one of the most popular male-only schools in Homs, the most iconic mosque, the largest stadium in the city and the road that connects Homs with its suburb, the New Homs, also known as Al-Waer neighbourhood.

Homs has its Old City, which was walled with seven gates. Its wall was made from black stones. Its remaining parts still stand in the city's urban landscape. Small and narrow alleyways and streets with traditional courtyard houses and palaces formed the Old City. In the south-west corner of the Old City is a hill on which stood an ancient citadel. The hill is at the heart of Homs, but unlike other citadels in Syria, such as the Citadel of Aleppo or Krak des Chevaliers, most of Homs's Citadel was lost long before the war. Until 1800, Homs remained mainly within the wall except for some cemeteries outside it. Throughout the end of the Ottoman era in Syria, the city started slowly expanding beyond the wall, with new souks being opened in the north, west and south of the city. This urban growth continued in Homs at the time of the French Mandate in Syria during 1923–46.

The increasing growth was accompanied by a change in the urban fabric of the Old City. In the first decades of the twentieth century, for instance, the city's buildings and structures started being removed to enable new sites. In 1920, stones from the Citadel were removed to be used in other parts of the city, and in the same year one of the Old City's gates was removed. Two other gates were removed in 1925. At the end of the French Mandate in 1946, a number of urban plans were proposed for Homs, one of them designed by a Polish planner. Such proposals were criticized for neglecting the social and cultural fabric of the city and its people (Al Masri and Al Saja n.d.). For several decades, internal migrants moved from the rural areas around Homs to the city. Whilst Homs was expanding as a response to this migration, its growth has been built on geographies of inequalities. New neighbourhoods started to emerge, often with poorly developed infrastructure and building services and a lack of open and green spaces. One of these neighbourhoods is called Al Muhajireen (meaning 'The Migrants') in reference to those who settled there.

Little has been written about the urban growth of Homs during the past century and I have struggled to find rigorous resources about the transformation of the city. At the university in Homs, there were no history, archaeology or sociology departments (unlike Damascus), and in the architecture department little has been done to conduct research on the city's urban growth. Homs has also been neglected when compared to Damascus and Aleppo which attracted research grants from national and international organizations, so the politics of representation may also have contributed to the lack of interest in writing about the history of the city from an urban perspective. Saying that, there have been rich studies that document the history of Homs more broadly, such as explorations in traditions, festivals, values and architecture. For instance, Naeem Salim Al-Zahrawi, a well-known historian of Homs, wrote about the rich architecture of the Old City, but not about the urban growth of the city.

The only paper I found on the urban growth of the city in the past century was co-authored by Emad Al Masri, a professor at the University of Damascus, and Hiba Al Saja (n.d.). In their paper, they bring together the different plans, proposals and visions for Homs and its growth during the past century, including proposals that emerged since the 1940s, such as the proposal of a Polish planner for the development of Homs between 1966 and 1975 and the plans of the Municipal Administration Modernization (MAM). Al Masri and Al Saja examined these plans which have shaped Homs and explored their limitations, such as the lack of understanding of the city's culture and identity, foreign interventions in planning the city with no respect to the social life and needs of the people, and the neglect of the city's history and its people's way of living. Whilst many would think that the destruction of Homs started in 2011, it is important to link the past decade's violence with the pre-war urban planning struggles and the losses the city and its people endured long before the revolution.

The destruction of Homs' markers of the past did not start in 2011, but decades before that. In her book, *The Battle for Home* (2016), architect Marwa Al-Sabouni dedicated an entire chapter to the Battle of Old Homs, and the defeat of the old by the new. In that chapter, Al-Sabouni described the Old City as a 'living museum of ancient architecture, but its treasures were jumbled and neglected, like dusty jewels at the bottom of an abandoned drawer' (p. 33). She continued to describe the Old City, where the officials in charge there replaced large numbers of the old buildings with new tower blocks or car parks.

Similar to many cities around the world that lost much of their social fabric through waves of gentrification, Homs too has lost much of its architecture and history. Since the 1980s, many traditional homes and historical palaces were demolished in the name of modernization and development. This includes homes that were built around the historic Citadel of Homs. Slowly and gradually, the Old City lost most of its characteristics and many of its demolished buildings were replaced by newly built, giant governmental and administrative blocks, and residential buildings were replaced by car parks. The year 1985 witnessed significant losses to the Old City as a large part within and around its north-west corner was razed to the ground in order to construct a new city centre that included high-rise buildings. The new city centre included buildings of over ten floors in an area where most buildings had one to three floors. Among these giant blocks were the offices of the Syrian Engineers Syndicate (Homs Branch), the Commercial Bank of Syria and Homs's City Council, as well as other buildings (Figure 1.1 and Figure 1.2).

The new city centre lacked green areas or open public spaces. One of the most dominant open spaces between these large buildings was turned into a

FIGURE 1.1 One of the remaining old buildings in Homs (*bottom left*), just outside the walled city of Homs, 2009.

Source: Ammar Azzouz.

(a) (b)

FIGURE 1.2 (*a*) Significant parts of the Old City of Homs were demolished in the early 1980s. (*b*) Remains of its wall still stand in these demolished areas, 2009.

Source: Ammar Azzouz.

massive car park near the wall of the Old City in the Bab Hud neighbourhood. Layers of memory have been erased with the demolition of architecture in the Old City, causing a loss to Homs' cultural heritage sites and architectural identity. Despite this loss, rich architecture still remained in the Old City which includes palaces, souks, hammams and old houses, but the Old City was neglected and abandoned to urban decay. The story of Homs that could have been told through its history, through its Old City, has gradually been lost. There have been few community-engagement programmes that introduced local people in Homs to their own cities through public events and debates. It felt that many who lived in Homs did not know its story, the buildings that made it, the streets that shaped it, or the richness of its social and architectural fabric. Even for architecture students in Homs, there was no course or trip or walking tour to the Old City.

Slowly, there was a sense of loss of the memory of Homs. This loss, however, was not only limited to the destruction and decay of the old building. In 2006, old acacia and eucalyptus trees had been removed from some of the streets in Homs, such as Al Ghouta Street. This was also the fate of the palm trees in Al Hamra Street as well as other streets in the city. Some of the palm trees were moved to other streets but most of them died. These tall trees were replaced by smaller and shorter ones, changing with them the image of these streets. Looking back at it now, it feels as if the city was redesigned to prepare for a war, to make these streets wide enough for tanks, and to clear the views from the trees for the snipers to kill. During the past decade, the towers that were constructed before 2011 turned into sites for snipers, turning them into 'Death Towers'.

Whilst Homs has been the victim of domicide since 2011, violence against its built environment has been slowly reshaping the city from before then. Pre-2011 urban renewal projects proposed erasing parts of the city rather than repairing or retrofitting them. The decade before the revolution witnessed the emergence of urban renewal plans to change Homs and destroy more of its old fabric in the name of modernization and development.

Despite the anger that many residents felt at the time of these emerging urban renewals, little was done to stop these radical changes to the city. At the Architecture Department, there was no urban scholarly activism to support and stand in solidarity with impacted communities. No NGOs or academics created platforms to engage with the local population in shaping their own cities. Writing about the impact of these projects on local communities and the city was limited, if not absent. Souad Jarrous (2006) was one of the rare people who published a powerful article on the removal of the trees. In her writing, she uses the words 'assassination' and 'massacre' to describe the removal and loss of the trees, explaining their importance for the city, as if they were residents in Homs. In her article, Jarrous reflects on an interview that was conducted with architect Farah Joukhadar. Joukhadar emphasized the need to engage with impacted communities in a public debate so that people are part of shaping their own city. Joukhadar stressed that this engagement is needed in any future project so that the 'tragedy', as in the case of the removal of the trees, does not occur again. These reflections were very important at the time, and are very important today, when people feel they are the last to be consulted about the future of their cities.

Jarrous' attention was not only directed towards the trees but also towards the emerging visions of Homs' future. This included the proposal to demolish some of the historic buildings in the city, such as the Soubhi Shoaib Fine Art Centre which was (and still is) one of the main destinations for artists, writers, musicians and intellectuals. I still remember the hours I spent at this art centre, the cosy atmosphere there, the ageing walls of the building. People would spend long hours each week drawing, painting or making sculptures. It was a rare place in Homs that attracted people from all around the city and from different backgrounds, sects and ages. The space was small and intimate. There were two rooms opening to each other where we all sat, almost shoulder to shoulder. Attendees built friendships there, and I made very good friends with people from different backgrounds and ages. Art brought us all together in a place full of creativity. Unlike other places in the city, the Soubhi Shoaib Fine Art Centre reflects the heterogeneity of Homs, and this very notion of heterogeneity is what has been targeted by the forces of domicide since 2011.

Once you enter the building and walk up the steep staircase, you smell the oil paints and hear classical music or the songs of the famous Lebanese singer, Fairouz. The pace of life was so slow there, staring for hours at objects on the table, or sometimes for a life drawing session. Each of us would draw this differently and with different techniques and materials, from coal and pencil to oil, pastel and acrylic. On the ground floor, and through its exhibition space, a door takes visitors to a courtyard which feels as if you have been transported to a different city. It was so peaceful there. I remember this place so vividly. How much we needed a place to bring us together then. And how much we need these spaces today that unite us despite our different stories and narratives. When the many buildings were demolished, complete layers of history and memory were erased, causing collective nostalgia to a city that was gradually vanishing. But it was not the case for the Soubhi Shoaib Fine Art Centre. This specific building was eventually preserved after local outrage. I emphasize here this specific building because it holds so many memories and is so significant in the minds of many Homsis, and in my own identity and upbringing. I also wanted to emphasize it because when we hear about domicidal reconstruction of Syria, we never hear about the meaning and significance of these lost architectures.

In the name of modernization and urban renewal, cities around the world are shaped and transformed by waves of destruction and displacement, and Homs is by no means exceptional. Ekaterina Mizrokhi (2021) has written about the demolition of cities in the time of 'peace' with a focus on Moscow. In 2017, the Municipality of the Moscow announced the demolition of several thousands of Soviet-era, standardized apartments in order to replace them with new residential districts that are marked as modern. Although the project is known as 'The Renovation', it involves no actual renovation. Rather, it suggests demolishing whole swathes of the city with no plans for its repair or retrofit. Whilst the municipality justifies the demolition by framing the targeted district as 'outdated', Mizrokhi argues that by doing so, this justification neglects, silences and displaces many of the existing residents whose attachment to their own neighbourhood is threatened by the demolition proposal. In Mecca, the birthplace of Islam, new internationally acclaimed luxury hotels, malls and designer-serviced apartments inside concrete skyscrapers have replaced the demolished spaces and places. The early 2000s witnessed the demolition of its thousand-year-old topography, including sacred and historic sites in Central Mecca. Cranes dotted the sky around the Grand Mosque (Masjid al-Haram) and much of Islam's material history, including places of religious significance such as the Prophet's birthplace, were destroyed (Bsheer 2020).

Whilst governments 'justify' the demolition of buildings and the displacement of people in the name of modernization and urban renewal, these projects might hold within them political and economic agendas that benefit the rich and elites and further marginalize already marginalized groups. In 'Elite Avenues', Stephen Graham (2018: 527) explains how some cities fetishize elevated highways or flyovers as part of their race towards 'globalness', but explains how such projects contribute to 'social segregation and secession within and between cities which privilege the mobilities of the privileged'. Similarly, in Homs, new urban projects have benefitted the rich and created segregating lines across the city, as I will explain in the next section.

Space of inequality

Homs was gradually changing. A series of projects were proposed for some of the major sites of the city. They emerged in 2007 as part of the vision of Mohammed Iyad Ghazal, the governor of Homs during 2005–11. Ghazal introduced 'The Homs Dream' project, which quickly became known by many in the city as the 'Homs Nightmare'. The project called for the destruction of several parts of the city in order to lay the foundations for newly built high-rise buildings that erased the social, cultural and environmental fabrics of Homs. The mayor at the time invited investors from the Gulf and other countries in the hope that Homs would be of interest to them for property and real estate investments. Deals were already signed with Qatari investors to work on the project (Aks Alser 2007). Members of the impacted communities called the project the 'Qatari Solidere', in reference to Qatar's interest in the project and the Solidere project, which destroyed different parts of Beirut's city centre during the post-war reconstruction (Nagel 2002; Ragab 2011). The aftermath of Solidere's reconstruction in Beirut continues to shape the city today as it turned its city centre into a disconnected geography within Beirut. It became in the past few decades a destination for wealthy residents and tourists whilst creating a space of exclusions to many residents who felt like strangers in their own city.

Despite the opposition to the project, Ghazal continued his efforts to promote it. In 2010, Ghazal met with Philippe Marini, a former member of the Senate of France, and made an analogy between the project in Homs and the Grand Paris projects. Indeed, the Homs Dream also had a version for the Grand Homs that included not only projects within the city itself, but also different parts of the Homs Governate such as Palmyra. At the meeting, Ghazal explained how Homs could be an attraction for French investment, especially in infrastructure and building projects in Homs, that might include transport and highway projects. Whilst some had seen in this vision an ambitious project for the future of Homs, others had concerns and fears that this Homs Dream would be built on crushing the dreams of the urban poor.

The Homs Dream also included two projects to be implemented in the orchards in the west of Homs: the 'People's Garden' and the 'Paradise of Homs'. The first was supposed to be a public garden in the city, whilst the second introduced entertainment buildings. This was a continuation of past plans that emerged in the 1990s. In 1994, the western orchards of Homs were forcibly acquired from their owners. Their land was supposed to be turned into the 'People's Garden' (part of the Homs Dream). On the land that stretched out across 462 acres lived 1,500 people, most of whom worked in these orchards and made their living from their land. These orchards were known as Homs' lungs as they formed a green belt on the western side of the city. They were, however, threatened as they were targeted for investment and development plans. The urban plans in Homs were pushing the poor towards extreme levels of poverty whilst further benefitting the few rich.

To enable the development of Ghazal's vision of the Homs Dream, the plan was to destroy several buildings, including many local shops at the heart of the city. People who lived or worked on the sites of the Homs Dream were supposed to be expelled from their homes, including the 1,500 people who lived in the orchards. One of the richest businessmen in Homs told these families that it was useless for them to plant tomatoes in these orchards when their land was worth millions if investments were made to build on it. Some of the orchards had already been removed to enable the construction of new wide roads, which were rarely used. Many families were impacted by the construction of these roads, and their orchards were cut down with little compensation for their loss. It was noted that in order to construct these roads, over 500 trees were removed, some of them were as much as 200 years old (Aljaml 2007).

Several public protests were organized as a response to the Homs Dream. I refer here to two of them. In November 2007, the people of the orchards, both men and women, took four vehicles and travelled to Damascus to deliver a statement to the Republican Palace and the Prime Minister. The second protest was in 2008 in the city centre of Homs, on the site that was threatened by demolition. In their statement, titled 'The Nightmare Reality of the Homs Dream', the families who travelled to Damascus explained their concerns and fears about the project. The only photo that I found from these peaceful protests was of women holding a banner saying, 'Our Homsi orchards are mixed with our sweat and the sweat of our ancestors, so don't make it mixed with our blood' (Zaman al Wsl 2007). This sentence means that the families were talking about their own heritage, and all the work they had done in the orchards. They also mentioned their blood, making an analogy that they would resist being removed from their own homes and lands and could only be removed if they were killed. In the Homs Dream, they found themselves uprooted and their homes and lands taken from them to be replaced by golf clubs and skyscrapers. They were promised compensation, but they explained that what they were offered was less than a tenth of the value of their lands and homes.

Little has been done to document and write about these protests and the grassroots activism. Today, it is so important to trace the story of those who rose against megaprojects that threatened people with displacement and dispossession. When objections to the projects started spreading across the city, the mayor asked why people did not come to object and provide their feedback in 2005 (Zaman al Wsl 2007). Many in Homs resisted the project and turned to legal processes to stop the project through collective action such as peaceful protests. One Syrian activist I spoke with told me that these forms of protests took place in 2005, 2006 and 2007 (Zaman al Wsl 2007). I was eighteen at the time of these protests, and I cannot remember them being covered in the news media. Furthermore, since protests in the city were prohibited, people may have avoided talking about them out of fear. Having said that, there was a lack of transparency about the project and little was done to engage with local communities in Homs.

The Homs Dream was officially launched on a larger scale at the Damascus International Fair in 2010. A report on the launch of the project was published and framed as a reflection on the government's process of development and modernization, so the mayor wanted to show that the project was not only his own vision, but was also a reflection of the national plans for urban policies in Syria. The report highlighted the importance of the project and how it would bring tourists from inside and outside the country, how it would create new economic opportunities and how it would improve the living conditions of the people through the development of the infrastructure system in the city and the creation of jobs in different sectors of the economy. These visions of worlding and modernizing Homs were seen as a threat to many Homsis. They saw in the project a threat to their way of living, a threat that would destroy Homs' urban fabric, one that would establish the foundations for supporting new economic elites and powers rather than benefitting the people who resided and worked in the area. The project was also criticized for its attempts to re-engineer the demographic population in the areas to replace and displace current residents with other communities from different neighbourhoods. Despite the opposition to the project, many of those who were not impacted by it, as well as those who were benefitting from it, saw in the Homs Dream an opportunity for improving the urban life in Homs.

As part of the 'Development and Modernization' movement that had been sweeping the country since 2000, different aspects of the way of life have been impacted, enabling with it the emergence of a new bourgeois in Homs. Families from wealthy backgrounds were able to afford a different way of living, study abroad, travel across the world and reside in villas, creating their own social and economic circles whilst disconnecting from the urban poor and middle-class communities. Wealthy residents in Homs opened and owned new restaurants and cafes, as in Al Hamra Street, and established new private schools and universities that were unaffordable to most of the people in the city. In this new 'developed and modernized' world, a new lifestyle was encouraged so that people looked 'modern' and 'developed' to fit in, very often disconnecting themselves from the rest of the city's inhabitants, whom they considered as 'unmodern' and 'undeveloped'. Some of these elitist wealthy circles looked down on the other communities who came from different sects and economic backgrounds. They discriminated against them and refused to see others outside their elitist bubbles. The marginalized people were getting further pushed to the margin, whilst the wealthy were getting wealthier and wealthier.

It was a struggle for many people to feel they could belong to this new Homs, especially those who come from not so well-known family backgrounds. In a city where neighbourhoods were named after selective families, such as Job Al Jandaley (Al Jandaley is one of the families in Homs), and where people would refuse friends or partners from other 'less-important' or 'less-known' families, it was painful to live through the discrimination and humiliation experienced by many people who believe they are the 'children of the homeland'. I had friends switching their accents on and off at the university so they could feel they would be accepted. Accents were markers for class and origin. All this struggle was also reflected in architecture and urban plans to benefit the rich and neglect the suffering and needs of the less affluent citizens of Homs.

At the time when selective and targeted areas were undergoing a transformation to attract and benefit the rich in the city, other neighbourhoods were neglected. The urban poor were left behind in neighbourhoods that lacked basic amenities. Inequalities widened between people and neighbourhoods. As bars and restaurants opened for the rich and wealthy, many residents struggled to afford having a coffee in them, feeling that the city is not built for them but for the few. Very often they were looked down upon by those of wealth. Communities lived separated in the city as if there were several cities within the city. People went to their local schools in neighbourhoods that were divided not only along sectarian lines, as in many neighbourhoods in Homs, but also along lines of income. Many thought that we lived together, but in reality this togetherness was built on grounds of othering, inequalities and injustice. These were the invisible walls.

Most people went to their local schools and grew up with students who mostly came from one sect or religion and similar social income backgrounds. Only very few schools in the city attracted students from across the different neighbourhoods. One of them is Al Basil High School for Outstanding Students, created by the Ministry of Education which opened such schools in a number of cities in Syria. The school brought together students from different sects and religions and from different social incomes and geographies, based on the intellectual abilities of the students and after passing different sets of exams to join this school. Unlike most secondary and high schools in Homs, this school was mixed gender (all elementary schools and universities in Syria are mixed). In segregated areas, children and teenagers in Homs would grow up surrounded by students from similar backgrounds and those who never went to university might rarely interact with people from other communities in their everyday lives. But this was not the case in Al Basil, where students from different communities came together, for example Alawites, Sunnis, Shia, Ismailis and Christians. Inequality intersects.

The exclusion that many students faced there was not based on sectarian lines but on social backgrounds with a class dimension. A number of other schools also attracted students from across the city and from different sects, including Al Ghassaniah Orthodox School, founded in 1887. These schools, however, were private and, unlike Al Basil School, attracted only the middle class and the richest of the city. The schools tell us the story of Homs. There were different communities who lived in the city, but many of them would never meet or interact with one another. Students who study in their local school until the age of eighteen might meet people from other sects and interact with them for the first time when they start their university. The schooling system reproduced inequality and sustained divisions between people of the city.

Whilst some neighbourhoods in Homs were mainly dominated by one sect, others were much more mixed and diverse. For instance, Al Kussur, Baba Amr and Al Tawzee Al Ijbari were made up of mainly Sunni communities, and Akrama and Al Zahra were made up of mainly Alawite communities. The Al-Waer neighbourhood that was built outside Homs, known as the New Homs, attracted communities from different sects and religions, including Christians and Muslims. These communities lived together in Homs, but many of them created their own narrative about themselves, whilst at the same time creating myths and stereotypes about the other. In *The Impossible Revolution: Making Sense of the Syrian Tragedy*, Yassin al-Haj Saleh (2017) notes that each group has developed its own narratives of superiority and victimhood. The construction of these narratives has been built on ancient and modern reference stories, victimhood and pieces of history. He adds that each group views itself as superior in their manners, modernity, secularism or religion.

Whilst divisions have continued in Homs to this day, the city should not be seen as exceptional. There is a growth in racial and class segregation, sectarianism and divisions within places, communities and states globally, and the practices of bordering in the everyday spaces is not limited to Homs, but also occurs in many other countries in the world (Hårsman and Quigley 1995; Calame and Charlesworth 2011; Marques 2015). Mike Morrissey and Frank Gaffikin (2006: 875), who research the impact of sectarianism on spaces, note that: 'cities marked by the sectarian geographies of ethnic enclaves demonstrate a complex relationship among space, place and identity formation. Most obviously in contested places, space can be, in part, a canvas inscribed with recurrent chapters of rival narratives and grievance, evoking a sense of two populations co-habiting one city yet occupying parallel universes.'

We can see this today in Syria with different parallels in lives within the same country and even within the same city. As divisions continue in cities around the world, where 'othering' continues to shape cities from London and New York to Johannesburg and Nicosia, there is an increasingly growing literature on the need to create more inclusive, hospitable, welcoming and safe cities for all communities (Doderer 2011; Catterall 2015; Lange-Maney and Weier 2019). These studies have focused on different lenses such as creating cities that respond to the ageing populations and making cities safe for women. The future of Homs and other cities should reflect on the different communities that live there and architects must play a critical role in engaging with these communities to deal with such differences in a different manner. This will depend on the willingness of architects to communicate with the people they are supposed to serve, rather than proposing designs that neglect the richness and diversity of the communities that live in Syria.

Widening gap between architects and communities

Before the war, there was a wide gap between architects and local communities. This gap was shaped and influenced by the teaching methodologies at the school of architecture that failed to encourage students to collaborate and engage with the communities for whom they are designing. In Homs, there was only one university, Al-Baath University, with its Department of Architecture. For several years, students are taught about architecture as if it was separate from people. By doing so, students saw the aesthetics of buildings and urban spaces as a priority whilst at the same time neglected the challenges and struggles people face in their own cities, such as widening injustices and increasing suffering and destruction.

Students were disconnected from the hopes, dreams and aspirations of the local communities. However, it is important to note that this disconnection between education and local communities is a challenge that evokes more universal tropes about architectural education in the majority of countries.

During their five-year course in Homs, students were rarely taught about the history of Homs and its contemporary urban life. Even those who studied at the time of the Homs Dream were not introduced to the project or encouraged to think about its impact on the city. In Design studios, academics would very often give projects to students with 'imaginary' lands instead of dealing with real sites. Students had no restrictions with these imaginary lands. Even when they were given a specific site in the city, students were encouraged to propose whatever they wanted on the site, such as starting from ground zero, suggesting mass demolitions, and designing buildings and spaces that did not mirror the social, cultural and urban life of Homs. Whilst many would argue that these were only architectural drawings on paper, they were making an impact on these students, who are the future architects of Homs, and who might continue with what they were taught after their graduation.

The Department of Architecture faced different challenges. The teaching practice by many academics was authoritarian, interventionist, sexist and aggressive, and the department was a site of unchallenged violence. Some academics humiliated students and played an authoritarian role as if they were mini dictators. Architects reported that several academic staff would enter the design studio, shout at the students and tear up their design drawings if they did not approve of them. One academic criticized a man for wearing narrow jeans, and on another occasion shouted at women for the way they dressed or put on make-up. This academic, who has shaped parts of the Homs Dream, kept shouting at one of my classmates, humiliating her and asking her why she did not cry whilst he was discriminating against her and harassing her. His authoritarian personality was also reflected in his approach when it came to the design, planning and governance of Homs. Students, due to their fear of their lecturers, would struggle to propose design projects that would not fit the architectural style desired by these academics. So, the school that was supposed to be the site of free and creative academic thinking, was another site of oppression (this is also linked to the kind of politics of the country).

The imaginary lands that students were given in their design studios have suddenly turned into real lands but with people whose lives will be impacted. This disconnection from the reality and the way students were taught architecture was not only damaging the city before the war but will also cause further harm in the future reconstruction. In 2021, in an interview with an architect in Homs, I was told by him that most graduation projects assigned by academics that year were focused on tourism projects, rather than on rehabilitation or reconstruction. 'Tourism? Now?' I asked him. 'At a time when over half of the population is displaced?' This reflects a complete disconnect from the struggle of Homsis and Homs and what is happening in the country more broadly. At a time when people are living in miserable conditions, the focus is on tourism instead of reconstructing people's homes.

At Al-Baath University in 2011, students and academics stopped talking to one another, or at least edited and filtered what they could talk about. It would be very clear from a brief conversation between staff and students to understand on which side each person stood. The university itself was a contested space as both staff and students were reporting their colleagues, who sympathized with the revolution. One lecturer I interviewed from his exile told me that he was reported multiple times by his fellow colleague and that there were multiple warnings for him to remain silent or leave the country. He eventually left Syria. Academics and students were at risk and the department which was supposed to be the safe space for free speech and intellectual criticism, was the site of violence. On 16 October, a peaceful demonstration in Homs was targeted. Two children and an architecture student, Taher Al Sebai, were killed. Taher's friend at the university commented on the loss of Taher before students entered their lecture. On the same day, the student was arrested after one of his classmates reported him. It was a matter of life and death; trust was broken. The university did not plan or organize any event to enable students to grieve the loss of their fellow student and friend. Despite the risk of arrest, many students organized a moment of silence at the entrance to the Department of Architecture on 20 October 2011.

Academics are an important group who contribute to the imagination and representation of cities. This group in Homs, however, was divided and under threat. Until now, there is no single academic inside Syria talking publicly in support of the revolution or providing any critical reflection on everyday life in the city. The dissent that took place in Homs came at a high price. Several staff members who were teaching in Homs have fled and started a new life abroad. Others, who before the revolution were sponsored by the university in Homs to continue their studies abroad and return to teach at Al-Baath University, decided to remain in countries such as Germany, UK, China and Russia. In their exile, several organizations have offered support to academics fleeing wars and conflicts such as the Scholars at Risk network that protects scholars and the freedom to think, and the Council for At-Risk Academics (CARA) that supports exiled academics. CARA has a specific programme focused on Syria, and by September 2020, 200 Syrian academics were actively engaged with it. Still, many Syrian academics have continued their careers abroad without the support of such organizations. The displacement and oppression of academics, especially the more critical voices, have contributed to maintaining the hegemony of some of the planners and architects. Their absence has also meant losing the opportunity to provide the new generation of architects with new planning theories, new modes of teaching and new ways of looking, thinking and writing about architecture.

Space of protests

From their televisions in Syria, people followed the protests in Tunisia in 2011. Syrians wondered if the wave of uprisings that was sweeping across many Arab countries would reach Syria. Activists and intellectuals in Homs started meetings to organize protests that started in Syria in March 2011. They found inspiration in other countries as they saw people gathering in public squares as part of what became known as the Arab Spring. Local communities in Homs started protesting in their own local neighbourhoods, searching for a small crossroad or a street where they could protest. The government increased the number of informants in public spaces, and in cafes such as Sobhi Shuaib, Al-Farah and Al-Rawda where activists would exchange ideas about the revolution. CCTV cameras were installed in different parts of the streets, including the city centre, in order for the government to control and prohibit any gathering in the heart of the city. Whilst Homsi communities continued their protests across different parts of Homs, they also wanted to gather collectively at Homs' main square, similar to what they saw happening in other cities such as in Cairo in Tahrir Square (Said 2015). Reaching the main New Clock Square in Homs was a challenge, as people were fearful of arrests and of being killed (Figure 1.3).

However, it was not long before people reached the New Clock Square. On 25 March 2011, both pro- and anti-government gatherings faced each other. Each chanting their own slogans. That day, anti-government protestors were calling for the mayor, Mohammed Iyad Ghazal, to step down, the same mayor who was promoting the Homs Dream project. However, the biggest moment that Homsis were waiting for happened in the afternoon of Monday, 18 April 2011. It was a symbolic date for Homsis, following a day when people had been killed in a peaceful protest in Bab Al-Sebaa, in the east of their city. It also represented a symbolic date for Syria with the first sit-in staged in the country.

On 18 April, shops in the city centre closed in a collective unplanned strike. At the Nuri Mosque, one of the ancient mosques in the Old City, prayers were recited for those who lost their lives on the previous day. The imam gave instructions on where to march and asked people not to chant anything sectarian, but this in itself shows how the fear of sectarian tensions was considered from the very early days of the revolution. The mourners marched

FIGURE 1.3 The Clock Tower Square, Homs, 2010.
Source: Ammar Azzouz.

in the streets towards the Al Hameediye neighbourhood and then to the Al Kathib Cemetery where those who had been killed in the demonstrations were buried. It is also a historical cemetery where several Companions of the Prophet Muhammad were buried. The march turned into a protest, a pattern that shaped most of the funerals at the start of the revolution. Following the funeral, mourners marched towards two key locations: the Khalid ibn al-Walid Mosque and the New Clock Square. Anger was on the rise, and many felt it was the turning point for Homs, that it was the time to be at the heart of the city, to reclaim it, to mourn the dead, to say that the wall of fear has been broken.

Thousands of people from different sects and religions, gender and age marched from across the city to their sit-in at the New Clock Tower. At this central public space, people chanted for dignity, freedom and justice. They also chanted the famous slogan that swept across cities during the Arab Spring as in Yemen, Bahrain, Tunisia, Libya and Sudan: 'The people want . . .,' and to it, they would add their demand (Achcar 2013). People climbed up the steps that surround the clock tower, holding the Syrian flag and formed a kind of pyramid, with people melting into one another. Gatherings in public squares were powerful because they showed the scale of the uprising and the power of the people who felt their voices were stolen from them, that their city is not for them to claim. Hopes were so high. This was the moment that would lead to a radical change such as the ones seen in other countries. But by the end of the day, the peaceful gathering was targeted and the sound of bullets spread across the city like a rain storm. The smoke of guns was in the air. Many people were killed on that night, many injured and many went missing.

It was a turning point in the Syrian Revolution: 18 April 2011. The events of that day became known as the 'Clock Massacre'. The square became known as the Freedom Square and the clock tower became a revolutionary symbol. But the loss endured in this square and the brutality which was faced by a peaceful protest did not stop people in Homs from protesting in their local neighbourhoods (Figure 1.4). Their persistence, resistance, momentum and courage had gradually led Homs to be known as the 'Capital of the Revolution', when lesser protests were taking place in other cities. Very soon after the anti-government demonstration that were met with arrests, killing and violence, a pro-government gathering took place at the same site, around the clock tower, and of course, nobody was harmed. It was the same place where the Homs Dream was proposed, so another layer of meaning was added to the square.

The site represents the struggle for the right to the city and the right to march and protest in the city centre. The site, however, was not only a representation of an individual's right, but was also a reflection of the collective struggle in Homs. As David Harvey (2008) notes, 'the right to the city is far more than the individual liberty to access urban resources: it is a right to change ourselves by changing the city. It is, moreover, a common rather than an individual right since this transformation inevitably depends upon the exercise of a collective power to reshape the processes of urbanization.' For

FIGURE 1.4 Women protesting in Homs, 31 October 2011.
Source: Given to the author with a request for anonymity.

protestors, this space was the representation of their collective power to shape the urban revolution in Homs.

With the absence of critical local and international journalists inside Syria, 'citizen journalists' emerged during the past decade. People documented and shared their reports and films with the world via their mobile phones and cameras. But despite the many films about the Clock Massacre, little to this day has been written about the square and its importance. An exception can be found in the work of Wael Rihani (2020), a writer from Homs who is currently based in Istanbul. In his article, he reads the square through the lens of time. To do so, he observes the different events that took place in this specific square across time. Rihani documents the symbolic meaning of the square and pays attention to the day of the massacre, 18 April 2011. He published several important articles documenting his life in some of the besieged areas before he fled to Türkiye. His writing is important, especially when the narrative about Syria is stolen from us and redirected to whitewash the suffering of the people.

In one of his most powerful articles, Rihani (2020) wrote about the memory of the New Clock Tower sit-in. It is a memory that Rihani, and many Syrians, reclaim each year to mark the anniversary of the sit-in and the massacre that took place on that day. Titled 'Ten Minutes to Twelve', Rihani's article evokes the memory of the massacre in order not to forget, in order to protect the story and the narrative. By focusing in the title on the minutes and the hour of the massacre, Rihani pays homage to this site and calls us to retell the story of Homs and its revolution. To fight amnesia, Rihani turns to writing as a vehicle to remember and as a tool to deal with the experience of exile that grinds our collective memory. Rihani adds that, although the voices of protestors are no longer in the square, their echo is still there, in the places that millions of people have been forced to flee. This echo is what Rihani calls us to remember, as we remember the ringing of the New Clock of Homs. Through his writing, he reconstructs a lost memory and draws our attention to the importance of this revolutionary site that is rarely researched and explored in studies on urban revolutions globally.

In other cities that witnessed mass protests in their squares, critical writings have emerged on the significance of these sites. In Egypt, for instance, several articles have been published on Tahrir Square in Cairo, raising questions on why the square evokes a symbolic meaning in the collective imagination of the people (Aboelezz 2015; Ziada 2015). Furthermore, analyses have been made to understand the spatiality of the Arab Spring as primarily an urban phenomenon where public spaces became the sites of hope and sociopolitical contestation (Lopes de Souza and Lipietz 2011; Kanna 2012). This can be seen in the important work of Nasser Rabbat (2012: 207), who writes about the link between the Arab Spring and public spaces in different cities such as Tunis, Cairo, Alexandria, Benghazi, Manama and San'a. He describes how people broke the chain of fear in revolting against corrupt regimes and how these squares 'virtually became their homes, their operation rooms, and our window on their revolution'. Today, we need more of these critical studies in the context of Homs and of Syria more broadly.

Since its construction and opening in 1964, the clock tower has had a significant meaning for the Homsi communities. For decades, it has been regarded as a symbol of Homs in the collective imagination of people (Table 1.1). It is built with black and white stones like the many buildings in Homs. The clock tower was funded by Kurjeyah Haddad in 1951, a Syrian woman who lived in Brazil. Haddad came to the official opening in 1964. This is why many people call this tower the Clock of Kurjeyah Haddad. The square is officially named Gamal Abdel Nasser Square because Nasser visited the site in 1960 when he was a president of Egypt. But for the local Homsis, it is better known as Al Tahrir Square (Liberation) or more commonly as the Clock Square. Before 2011, people marched to the square after football matches to celebrate, holding flags for the team they support and, historically, the square was the site that witnessed public gatherings and protests. The clock tower is cemented in the minds of the people, perhaps more than any other site or monument. Unlike religious buildings such as mosques or churches, the clock tower is a symbolic site in a way that many feel they can relate to more than to a religious building. Its location at the heart of the city adds another layer of importance as it is situated in the middle of a square. Many architecture students in the past have even proposed turning the site into a pedestrian square due to the lack of open public spaces in Homs and the significance of this site. When I spoke to Homsis about their memory, some told me that for them, it is like Big Ben in London.

The site always remained in the mind of many Homsis but was often unreachable. Attempts to protest there again were met with violence as in the attempts on 22 August 2011. Very soon afterwards, the government closed the main road that connects Homs' two clocks, the old and new clocks as they are known in the city. The city gradually started to be divided and broken up into pieces so that no mass protests could reach the heart of the city. After April 2011, anti-government protesters were no longer able to walk there. The site was reopened to the public in 2014. Since people have been prohibited to protest in the square, they started building replicas of the clock tower across different parts of the country, and even outside of Syria. The clock tower started to emerge as a centrepiece for protestors to imagine that they are reclaiming their right to the square. There is a saying about this: Wherever Homsis go, they take their Clock with them.

TABLE 1.1 Selected Dates and Events that Took Place at the New Clock Tower Square

Date	Event
August 1964	The New Clock Tower was opened.
25 March 2011	First large peaceful protest march towards the New Clock Tower Square, protestors called for changing the mayor of Homs and the fall of the regime.
18 April 2011	This date was a turning point in the history of revolution in Homs, which witnessed a large sit-in on the square, a day after the massacre there of nine men. The sit-in was targeted by the government.
22 August 2011	Protestors gathered in the square as an international organization was visiting Homs (UN), the protestors were targeted with guns.
September 2011–14	The square was besieged by the regime as the street that connects Homs' two clock towers was closed. No one was allowed to visit the site even if walking on foot.
27 December 2011	Protestors gathered in Al Khalidiya and many attempted to march to the square as a group formed by the Arab League was visiting Homs. The protesters reached the streets surrounding the square but were met with bullets and tear gas, and two protestors were killed. The protesters were unable to reach the square.

Space of war

With the start of the revolution, anger, fear and lack of trust started separating people from one another. This was the case from the very early months of the revolution. There were attempts by the government to fuel these fears and turn people against one another along sectarian lines. In Al Hadara Street, in a neighbourhood mainly of Alawite communities, a number of shops of Sunni owners were targeted and destroyed in July 2011. People stopped talking to one another. Divisions emerged between those who support the regime and those who support the revolution, others remained silent preferring not to take any side, at least publicly, in order to navigate across these divided communities; they were named the *grey layer*. The city began to be divided spatially through conflict infrastructure.

As public spaces became contested and targeted, conflict infrastructure started to emerge in Syria to block access to these sites and to prohibit people from gathering in the main squares of cities and villages. Walls, fences, buffer zones, cement blocks and barriers had been added to break up the built environment, to divide communities and to control access through checkpoints. People were questioned at checkpoints and asked to show their IDs. These physical dividing lines cemented the pre-war intangible divisions that separated people from each other through sectarian or social lines. Space was weaponized. As divisions restricted people's movements, each neighbourhood started to become like a city within the city. People relied solely on the local shops rather than visiting the city centre which was inaccessible. Some people remained in their local neighbourhood for years as they feared being arrested at a checkpoint, especially men who risked being forced to join the military.

In *Negotiating Conflict in Lebanon: Bordering Practices in Divided Beirut*, Mohamad Hafeda (2019: 26) explores 'the negotiation of positions, and of spatial practices as tactic and strategy, material and immaterial, within the space of the other' as a bordering practice. Borders, according to Hafeda, are part of the everyday spatial practices that 'socially and physically divide people while simultaneously connecting them'. To capture the material and immaterial divides, the social and the physical ones, Hafeda introduces at the start of his book a list of bordering practices such as hanging up political posters on buildings, painting the facades of buildings and shops in a party's political colours or flags, installing surveillance cameras and forbidding access to sites by blocking them with trash bins, sandbags and barbed wires. Hafeda incorporates in the list different bordering practices, including 'sound', which he introduces as an effective way to produce borders. Through speeches, firework and vehicles playing loud political songs, sound travels invisibly across divided sectarian geographies and becomes a substitute for physical population of space.

Almost all the bordering practices that Hafeda listed in Beirut have also been dividing communities in Homs, both socially and spatially. When areas were captured by rebels in Homs, shops and facades were painted with the revolution flag, and murals were painted with written messages of hope and resistance on the walls of buildings. When the government captured these sites, all the revolution markers in the space were erased. Space was then reshaped by painting the government's flags on shops across entire streets and installing posters and photographs to reflect the government's 'liberation' of these areas. Dividing borders emerged in Homs across neighbourhoods even when they were under the control of the government. However, these dividing lines were sharper and more extreme when separating government-controlled areas with rebel-held areas – as in the times of siege.

Movement to and from several divided spaces was restricted but still possible in government-held areas through checkpoints. This, however, was not the case of besieged neighbourhoods. The Syrian government has laid siege to multiple neighbourhoods across different times during the conflict – also across different cities and towns such as Damascus and Aleppo. Sieges have been used for military blockades, which meant a complete lack of access to food and medical supplies and movement. Waad Al-Kateab (a pseudonym) has filmed the everyday life in the city of Aleppo under siege where she resided with her family. In her documentary, *For Sama* – named after her daughter Sama who was born at the time of the siege – Al-Kateab brings millions of viewers globally to the everyday life of families under siege (Al-Kateab and Watts 2019; Azzouz 2020a). Gradually, Homs became divided. Most places that used to bring people together were segregated, like the city centre where the New Clock Tower and the old markets are. Communities were divided and unable to see one another or mix as they used to before 2011. One of the main spaces that kept bringing people together, however, was the university. But as one of the engineers I interviewed who lived in Homs said, if there were two public universities in Homs, people would have been divided.

During the past decade, cities and towns have become targeted, destroying the familiar and displacing their people. For over ten years now, more than half of the Syrian population has been displaced from their homes. Over 6.8 million people have fled Syria, seeking refuge in neighbouring countries, such as Türkiye, Lebanon, Jordan, Iraq, Egypt and beyond, whilst nearly 7 million people have been internally displaced within Syria. Across Syria, more than a third of the housing sector has been destroyed. Among the most impacted cities is Homs. Bombed, shelled, divided and several times partially besieged, the city of Homs has become synonymous with urban decay, destruction and ruins.

Destruction in Homs has led to the loss or damage of its symbolic architectural and cultural heritage sites, for example, the damage to Um Al Zennar Church (Church of Saint Mary of the Holy Belt), mosques (such as Khalid ibn al-Walid, Ka'ab al-Ahbar and Al Zawya), courtyard houses and covered historic souks. But this destruction was not limited to the monumental, the ancient and historic cultural heritage sites. Spaces and places of everydayness have been damaged, bombed, bulldozed and razed to the ground.

The built environment has been weaponized. Tower blocks became threats as snipers got ready to kill people. The Gardenia towers that were intended to be the most luxurious hotel in Homs, Gardenia Rotana Hotel (28 floors), and a residential building for the rich (21 floors), were still under construction when the war started. Due to their scale and location, the towers turned into sites of control to overlook the city and kill its people. The two towers stand at the edge of Homs as the tallest buildings in the city, and overview different parts of the city, including Homs' orchards and Al-Waer neighbourhood, which was besieged and targeted. For years, these two towers were weaponized and became known as the Death Towers.

Space of alienation

In the early months of the revolution, tanks entered Homs to destroy it. A few of them were bordering onto my own neighbourhood. Each day was a struggle: protests were targeted, people killed or injured, hospitals raided to arrest the wounded. Funerals turned into protests, which were attacked. The cycle continued. From our windows and balconies, we saw the bombs falling on Baba Amr. It was one of the many neighbourhoods in Homs that was destroyed. By 2014, over half of Homs' neighbourhoods have been destroyed, whilst 22 per cent of the neighbourhoods have been partially damaged (UN-Habitat 2014). Further destruction took place beyond that date, in particular in the Al-Waer neighbourhood, but this has not been documented in any recent damage assessment of Homs. The city that we used to know is no longer there.

Whilst the destruction of cultural heritage sites in Syria has attracted international attention, little has been done to highlight the toll of war on people who lost their homes. Since 2011, people's homes have been wilfully destroyed. Their stories of loss, trauma, nostalgia and grief are often lost in the discussions about conflicts and war. Jawad, who grew up in Homs and is now an architect volunteering in one of the local charities in Homs, told me about the pain he experienced when losing his home. His home was on the third floor, he told me after sending a photo of a ruined building on WhatsApp. His family returned to their ruined home to find it mostly looted, and whilst he narrated his loss of home, it also evoked the memory of lost times that seem far away from reality now.

Jawad remembered things that seem like another life for him now. It is that 'another life' that he recalled: the time when his family put their savings in this home, and the time that he, as an architecture student, designed his own bedroom. In that 'another life', it was not only about the material-built environment, but more importantly it was about the people, the sense of belonging created with the supporting networks that have been broken and destroyed. His school and neighbourhood friends are gone. Jawad worked in a charity that helps rehabilitate partially damaged homes, but his home requires more than rehabilitation. His family was unable to reconstruct their ruined home as the entire building might collapse. The economy in Syria has collapsed and most people are unable to afford rehabilitating or rebuilding their homes. With extreme living conditions, Jawad's family eventually decided to sell their home which is located at the heart of the city. They rented a flat on the edge of the city. Many people outside Syria are buying these homes as their currency is strong and stable. This displacement of people due to the lack of any form of support to reconstruct their home has an impact on the social fabric of the city. People are not only suffering the consequences of the destruction of their homes, but they are also being pushed to the edge to sell their homes and leave the ruins.

Jawad and his family only lived for one month in their home after his family bought it. He participated in designing and decorating his bedroom. But with the shift of the frontlines to his neighbourhood, Jouret Al-Shayah, they had to flee their home. After they left, it was attacked, and they felt obliged to sell as a matter of survival. Jawad expressed how he feels like a flower torn from its root and planted in a new place.

Due to the mass destruction in Homs, many people are feeling exiled in their own city. The familiar architecture is lost, the local shops are closed or replaced with new ones, whilst some of the areas are completely razed to the ground. In *The Destruction of Memory: Architecture at the time of war*, Robert Bevan (2006: 13) examines the impact of destruction on communities. He notes that, 'to lose all that is familiar – the deliberate destruction of one's environment – can mean a disorientating exile from the memories they have invoked. It is the threat of a loss to one's collective identity and the secure continuity of those identities.'

Many Homsis whom I spoke with expressed to me similar thoughts as they feel like strangers in their own city. Sameh is one of them. When I spoke with him in 2017, he was displaced internally as he moved with his family from the besieged Al-Waer neighbourhood to Al Dablan Street in the city centre. Sameh is an architect who was volunteering in one of the main local charities in Homs, working on different initiatives. He lamented the time in Homs before the war and how it used to pulse with life. It was nostalgia for a pace of life that no longer exists, for the people no longer around, for the architecture and the sense of tranquillity. He said that after having been amongst the ruins of Homs, he always thinks that everything can be lost in the blink of an eye. This loss is not only about the loss of tangible history, but also about the loss of the people who made the city.

Conclusions

It may appear to many that domicide in Homs started in 2011. But it did not. Domicide's roots and origins of demolition, sectarian and class segregation, forced displacement and divisions began long before the start of the Syrian Revolution. I argued in this chapter that 'peacetime' domicide was not the product of tanks and battlefields but, rather, it was the outcome of slow violence that weaponized architecture and urban planning. From the demolition of the Old City in Homs to the creation of unjust and unequal neighbourhoods, violence has made many Homsis feel that their city is not their own, that they are strangers in their own city.

This sense of exile and strangerness has continued over the past decade with the radical destruction of Home. The slow violence that gradually and slowly manifested itself in the city before 2011 has taken sharper and more extreme forms since the start of the revolution. The hidden lines that segregated and separated people in Homs before 2011, have literally turned into physical ones after 2011. The neighbourhoods of the urban poor were demolished and destroyed, whilst their people have been killed or forcibly displaced. Architecture and planning have been used as tools to transform Homs as a city into a battlefield. Many people today feel strangers in their own city, even those who remain in Homs. The familiar places and spaces have been wiped out, and many of the people they used to know are no longer around.

In this chapter, I attempted to link 'peacetime' domicide with wartime domicide. By doing so, the line between peace and war becomes more blurred. Wartime violence, hence, appears as a continuation and a radical expansion of 'peacetime' violence. Several scholars today research this very relationship between peace and war through the lens of architecture and urban planning. One of these scholars is Hiba Bou Akar (2019: 9), who focuses on Beirut in times of 'peace' and 'war' and since the end of the Civil War in Lebanon of 1975–90, when religious-political organizations have turned Beirut into frontier geographies to reflect their imagined role in local and regional wars yet to come:

> War in times of peace is not fought with tanks, artillery, and rifles, but through a geopolitical territoriant contest, where the fear of domination of one group by another is played out over such issues as land and apartment sales, the occupation of ruins, access to housing, zoning and planning regulations, and infrastructure projects.

Valérie Clerc (2014) has contributed to this knowledge in the Syrian context. In her work on informal settlements in Syria, she linked pre-war laws and decrees to the wartime destruction of informal settlements. As several informal neighbourhoods have been razed to the ground at the time of war, Clerc argues that this destruction can be seen by planners and inhabitants as wartime tools to accelerate urban renewal plans that the Syrian government established before the war. This destruction will now influence the future reconstruction project in Syria that might emerge as a new face of domicide, which I will explore in more detail in Chapter 5.

2

War on home

In search of a place to call home

I was living in a place which was affected by bombing and destruction. At some point, my family and myself had to leave our house, because it was threatened to be bombed. I remember that after we left our house, I think one week after, we heard it was destroyed. One of my friends heard that, and he told us that it was destroyed. At that time, the immediate idea that came to my mind was that we don't have a home any more, although we were in my uncle's house. I thought we were lucky, we had a home, we had another home, we were not living in the street or in camps or tents and we didn't have to leave the city immediately like some other people had to.

I was the first one to know that my house was destroyed. So, I was the one who was responsible to tell my mum and dad. So, I came to my mother and told her, 'What would you do if you knew that your house was destroyed?' She said, 'I would go crazy.' And I told her: 'It is destroyed.' Because, honestly, I couldn't find any easy way to tell her that. It had to be the hard way. There is no easy way. I had to tell her in that way.

Both my father and mother were devastated, the word I think, for around a week. We spent the whole week grieving. Then we were thankful that we were all safe, no one was harmed. I think that is the way we consoled ourselves, that we are safe. No one is injured. Everyone is safe and sound. And we thanked God we *weren't in our house when it happened. So, it took us around a week or so to recover from that shock. But my mum was always saying, 'I feel like I lost a piece of me because I lost my house.' Because it was her dream house, she and my father literally built that house and they bought everything new for it. So, I think she won't forget that.*

So at the beginning of 2011, we had to leave our house because the whole area was threatened to be either bombed or there was genocide. So, we left to my grandmother's house. Then we left to my uncle's house, then we left to some long-distance relatives in rural Damascus, then we went back to Homs to my uncle's house in late 2013, then we rented a house, then we had to leave to another house because of the bombing and after that we had to change four houses because the house owner wanted it. We changed ten houses in eight years.

OMAMA ZANKAWAN, LONDON-BASED CITIZEN FROM HOMS, INTERVIEW, LONDON, 2019

Loss of home

This is Omama Zankawan's story. It is a story of one of the more than 14 million Syrians who are displaced from their homes. Of them, over 6.7 million are Internally Displaced People (IDPs) inside Syria. At the end of 2020, the Internal Displacement Monitoring Centre reported there are over 55 million IDPs across the world. Syria has the largest internally displaced population. Zankawan moved from Homs to London in September 2018 to complete her postgraduate studies. She found a new home in London and never returned to Homs. In London, she has made friends and socialized, making a kind of new home for herself, thousands of miles from Syria. None of these new friends in her exile were aware that she had lost her home, and she kept this to herself, she later told me.

When I was conducting my research on domicide, I asked friends and connections if they know someone who has lost their home and is willing to talk to me about their own experiences of loss and displacement. Zankawan's friend who is based in Germany got in touch with me, suggesting that I speak to her friend, and so I did in 2019. One year after she left Homs, I met with Zankawan in London to listen to her story and to hear about the multiple internal displacements she endured before moving to the UK. Zankawan spoke to me about belonging, mourning and nostalgia for the home they have lost. She recalled the memory of lost home, the place her family called 'the dream house'. It was the dream they built after renting in Homs until she was seventeen, when her parents decided to put all of their savings in this new home they bought. She recalled, with a joking voice, how her father who had a background in mathematics, not in architecture or interior design, designed the interior of this home. 'This is why the corridor is larger than my bedroom,' she smiled, recalling that memory. It is this story of the dream house that Zankawan narrated to me. A dream house where Zankawan and her family were planning to build a better future for themselves. This sanctuary, this dream house is all gone.

Like Zankawan, many of the people I spoke with had to flee their homes for long periods of time before they were able to return. Some people left their homes for weeks, months, whilst others for years, hoping they would return, but they never did. During wartime, some IDPs might remain displaced from their homes for decades or their entire lifetime without being able to return home, as in the case of many refugees who live and die in their exile without being buried in the country they were forced to flee. The return of displaced people to live in the home they fled is only possible if it still physically exists and is not razed to the ground, and also if they are permitted to return by those political and military forces that control these areas. Zankawan who fled Syria in 2018 after being displaced from her home in 2011, told me she was never able to see her home in Homs where she resided, even seven years after being displaced inside Homs, and even though she was residing very close to her home. Millions of Syrians have been living in non-government-held areas for a decade now without being able to return to their homes.

Many of the people who were forced to flee were displaced at very short notice. Saleem, an architect in his early thirties, told me that their neighbourhood, Jouret al-Shayah, was targeted by bombs and shells that they had to flee at night. The sudden displacement makes people take the dangerous routes to flee their own neighbourhoods during shelling and to decide on the spot where to go next. At the same time, those who are forced to flee at short notice know that the return to their home might be impossible in the short term and hence, they need to think of what little they can take with them. Together with his family, Saleem had to take a car, so their capacity to take anything with them was limited. They took with them some valuables, their IDs, certifications and some clothes. His story is similar to that of the millions of people who have been displaced. Nataly is one of them. When I spoke with her in 2018, she told me that within the period of seven years, they had to change homes five times until her family decided to sell their home in Homs and settle down in the countryside. She told me that the people living in the entire building in Homs packed their bags overnight. It did not matter to them where they went as long as it was safe, but there was chaos everywhere. Nataly remembered what she and her family took with them: some clothes, money, passports, some of her artwork, gold and jewellery, letters, certifications and a small bag of souvenirs. She said she was keen to keep a memory of her home, even in that moment of chaos.

Displacement at very short notice has been experienced by many Syrians across different parts of the country. The Syrian government gave people very short notice in Hama to evacuate their homes and shops that later were demolished and bulldozed. This was reported by Human Rights Watch in interviews they conducted for their report, *Razed to the Ground* (HRW 2014). It is noted in the report that the Syrian Army used megaphones to tell the residents in Wadi al-Jouz that they had one hour to pack their belongings. In Damascus, residents reported that the army arrived in their neighbourhood unannounced, asking people to leave their homes immediately and threatening to detain all those who raised any questions. One of the interviewees reflected on the 50-day operation to destroy the neighbourhood, saying that:

> The army demolished 1,250 shops and 650 homes. Eighteen-hundred families had to evacuate. There were two or three families in every house. The Syrian army gave the shop owners 24 hours to empty their shops. Homeowners were given only three hours to pack their stuff and leave. It was not enough time. People barely took anything with them. (HRW 2014: 26)

Another interviewee who witnessed the destruction of yet another neighbourhood in Damascus said that:

> Owners were given one hour to evacuate their homes. I saw people throwing their belongings from the windows. I wanted to help but I was afraid because the Syrian army was there.

IDPs are among the most vulnerable displaced communities as the forces that caused their displacement continue to shape their everyday life. The changing dynamics of conflicts can lead people to multiple displacements within their own country as they search for safety. This has been the case for many people I spoke with. In Syria, there have been reports stating that some people have been displaced as many as twenty-five times in the past decade (Beaujolais 2016). Zankawan's family had been displaced ten times in eight years when I spoke with her in 2019, but her family's displacement continued after she left to the UK. Reports have documented that the Syrian government has unlawfully prevented the return of IDPs from former anti-government-held areas to their properties (HRW 2018). The government imposes restrictions to access neighbourhoods or entire towns.

In search of home

There are many reasons for the multiple displacements that IDPs endure. As in the first displacement for Zankawan, their neighbourhood, Al Khalidya, was targeted and there was a fear of mass killings being carried out there. Fearing for their lives and searching for safety, thousands of Homsis have been internally displaced as their neighbourhoods have been the sites of massacres, violence, sniper attacks, arrests, aerial bombardment and shelling. Al-Khalidiya, which is located on the north-east side in Homs is one of the most damaged parts of the city. As Zankawan noted, their home was destroyed just one week after they fled from it. The neighbourhood was one of the earliest parts of Homs that witnessed waves of displacement in 2011, mainly inside Homs, but also to Damascus and its countryside, before people started leaving Syria to go to Lebanon and other neighbouring countries. As people fled their neighbourhood, they went to stay with others, often finding shelter in the homes of their relatives or friends for varied periods of time. They might have been living as little as a 15-minute walk from their home, and yet were unable to access or visit it due to the fear and danger as their home was located inside a besieged and targeted neighbourhood. People have not been allowed to visit their homes that are located inside besieged areas until they were permitted by the Syrian government. Many displaced people prefer to stay close to their home in the hope they will be able to return.

In their search for a shelter inside Syria, IDPs have followed different approaches, influenced by different factors such as family ties, access to shelter, basic services and humanitarian needs, apparent safety, religious and ethnic affiliation and the powers that were controlling the areas to which they are moving. The patterns and types of displacement varied, and included camps, renting, collective renting, hosting, squatting, collective shelters or living in unfinished or partially damaged buildings. Some IDPs have even found refuge in the ancient ruins of the Dead Cities in the north of Syria (Hubbard 2021). One of the most dominant approaches to finding shelter, however, is hosting. Relatives and friends hosted individuals or families inside their own homes. Families hosted each other temporarily or long-term, turning their own flats into collective flats for multiple families. Each family would live in a room, whilst multiple families share the communal areas such as the kitchen and the living room. Hosting was mostly seen as a temporary shelter solution as many people thought their need to access shelter would only be for a short period of time. But when I spoke with people in 2021, many still resided in the home of their hosts. In 2014, the UN-Habitat's City Profile Homs report noted that hosting was the most dominant mechanism for IDPs to access shelter. Of the IDPs, 30 per cent at the time were hosted by families, friends and non-relatives. Some families relied on the kindness and generosity of their friends and relatives who have more than one flat, so they have been hosted there for free or with lower rental agreements and often without formal leases. Hani, who was 22 when I spoke with him in 2017, had to flee with his family from the siege of the Al-Waer neighbourhood. They first moved to the Al-Ghouta neighbourhood. Later, a family friend who had migrated to Saudi Arabia long before the revolution, gave his home keys to Hani's family to live there for free. The new home for Hani's family was in Al Dablan Street, in the heart of the city and near the New Clock Tower. And even when the siege of the Al-Waer neighbourhood ended, Hani's family preferred not to return as the area was damaged and the services in the heart of the city were relatively better than in Al-Waer. For their family friend in Saudi, having friends living in his empty house was also important as many homes were completely looted, whilst others became targets for squatters. This happened to many who fled their homes during the past decade. Every person I spoke to who still has their home intact inside Syria had asked someone they know to live in it. This was either an invitation to a friend or a relative, or to tenants, so that they could have some income. But in all cases, this approach helped those who fled Syria to keep their homes protected from looting and squatting. People helped people. They supported one another during the time of chaos. During the darkest times, and even with the individual and collective loss, they stood in solidarity with one another.

The City Profile report also highlights that the majority of IDPs were living in rented accommodation in 2014. With the loss of livelihood, the killing of family members and the struggle to access jobs, many families have been unable to afford renting a place of their own. There are families living in cohabitation, often in overcrowded apartments so they can pay the rent collectively. Many of the owners of these rented apartments have refused to enter formal rental agreements, favouring verbal agreements, which used to be common before 2011. This, however, increases the vulnerability of IDPs as they could be threatened with displacement by their landlords or landladies, whenever they wanted the flat and without sufficient notice to terminate their stay. In cities such as Homs that witnessed the mass destruction of homes, the demand for housing kept increasing in the relatively safer areas, not only because Homsis moved within Homs, but also because many others fled to Homs from different parts of Syria. At the same time, rent prices kept increasing rapidly because property owners would ask tenants for more payments within short periods of time. With the collapse of the economy and the loss of jobs and income resources, many families have been pushed into extreme poverty. The increase in rent, therefore, meant another cycle of displacement for families who search for cheaper and/or smaller apartments to rent in other parts of Homs or Syria.

Not everyone was able to find a host family to live with, especially when mass waves of displacement swept Homs. Hence, collective shelters emerged in the first few years of the conflict both in public and private buildings. Schools and churches opened their doors to host IDPs, whilst unused public and private buildings and exhibition halls, as in the Al-Waer neighbourhood, were turned into collective shelters. These collective shelters have in some cases been officially registered by the Ministry of Local Administration (MoLA). MoLA assigned some of the international non-governmental organizations (INGOs) to support IDPs in these registered shelters (UN-Habitat 2013). Often overcrowded, these collective shelters have hosted some of the most vulnerable IDPs. However, those who were unable to access collective shelters or get support from any friend or family member, have ended up in makeshift shelters on vacant lots with little or no access to basic needs. These are among the most vulnerable IDPs in Homs.

Impact of internal displacement on people

For those who are displaced multiple times, their relationship to objects, their attachments to belonging, change. Those who have lost their homes know that whatever they own, whatever they build, might be destroyed again in the blink of an eye. Zankawan expressed these dilemmas in her conversation with me. It is the fear of attachment, the shifting and changing attitudes towards life, towards belongings, towards possessions. It is the fear of loss, the constant loss, the fear of another destruction yet to come. She told me (London, 2019):

> we left Homs in 2012, we lived in rural Damascus for a year and a half. During that time, we rented another house, we furnished it, and we wanted to start over, but then again, we had to leave, and we went back to Homs. It was bombed again. So, I think that my mother lost two houses. So, after that, she decided she does not want to furnish any house, she doesn't want to buy any luxurious things because she was afraid it might be destroyed again.
>
> All of our mothers like the China set of tea and their glasses. They are precious to them. It wasn't that way any more. So, if we broke a glass, it was OK. Before 2011, it wasn't OK at all. This glass was precious for them, for my mum. But after that, it was another thing. It does not matter any more. Because they were afraid if I like this glass, at some point in the future, it might be destroyed or bombed again.

What Zankawan mentioned in our conversations is the grief for their lost home (see Box 2.1). She noted in my interview with her, how the entire family grieved when they knew that their home was destroyed. Whilst she recalled the events of telling her mother about the destruction, she revisited the words her mother said when she knew their dream home was lost: 'I feel like I lost a piece of me because I lost my house.' People who lost their home have often expressed to me the grief they endure. This is what Porteous and Smith refer to as the grief syndrome of domicide experienced by the suffering people who lost their home. In an online interview in 2018 with Nadia (who preferred to remain anonymous), who left her home in Homs in 2012 and moved to Mashta al-Helu before she fled to Germany in 2018, she was only able to revisit her home once. When she returned there before she left Syria, she and her family found their home destroyed. When I interviewed Nadia in 2018, she told me that she is unable to retell the story as it is very difficult for her to go through the traumatic memory again. But she briefly remembered this visit in 2014. She told me how much she cried. She was afraid in her ruined home, and decided never to return to see it again. As she spoke to me from Germany, she told me she avoids talking about Syria. She no longer wants to think about her home country as she did not feel like a human being in Syria, she added. Nadia told me she is trying to build a new life in exile whilst slowly erasing any trigger or trace of the difficult past. Whilst both Nadia and Zankawan told me about their loss years after the destruction, the loss they endured influences their relationship with the past, the present and the future. For Zankwan, it is the relationship she has with places that might be threatened to be lost again, and for Nadia, it is the attempt to bury the past and forget about an entire country in a struggle to deal with her own trauma.

> **BOX 2.1** Omama Zankawan's story of displacement and domicide, 2021.
>
> I remember that there were thousands and thousands of people, all walking towards Old Homs. We were all walking, there were no cars or vehicles. So, everyone was walking towards that area, the Old Homs (Figures 2.1, 2.2 and 2.3). It was so silent. No one was talking. No one. You can literally hear the pin when you drop it on the ground. We were all just astonished and amazed by the amount of destruction that was there. I have never seen anything like that in any movie or documentary about World War II. I have never seen that. It was all destroyed, completely, that area.
>
> So, first we went to my grandmother's house because it was in an area before our house (Figure 2.4). It wasn't all destroyed so we could find stuff and some things there. We spent about an hour. We were just standing there, and we didn't know what to do. The house was upside down. I don't know why. And then we decided that we wanted to go and see our house.

It was about 20 minutes' walk I think between my grandmother's house and our house. And there was a mountain of dirt and stuff so we had to climb it. It was about to get dark. So my mother refused. She said if we climbed it and we went to the other side, I don't know what is there. So, it would be dangerous for us to go there. So we didn't go. We didn't see our house at that time.

But later the piles were removed and the roads were clearer for people to walk in to go and see their houses in that area. Our relatives went and they took photos of the house. It was all burnt. My relatives said she was trying to find a little piece of our house to bring it back to us, but she couldn't. It was all burnt and destroyed. And I haven't seen it. We couldn't. We didn't go back and that area was closed. It was only opened for a brief time, then it was closed. So, we couldn't go there. I didn't see my house. We don't have any photo of the house before the destruction, any photo, not even for us. So, the only memory of the house is in our heads. In our minds.

Omama Zankawan (London, 2019)

FIGURE 2.1 Families march to the Old City of Homs after the end of its siege, 2014.

Source: Omama Zankawan, taken by S.Z.

FIGURE 2.2 A scene from the Old City of Homs after the end of its siege, 2014.
Source: Omama Zankawan, taken by S.Z.

In an online report, a journalist joined a woman searching for her home and reporting on the moment she realized her home had been reduced to rubble. In 2018, Alex Thomson, the Channel 4 News journalist, visited the Yarmouk Camp, the largest Palestinian camp in Syria at the end of its five-year siege and bombardment by the Syrian, Russian and Iranian forces (read Hanan's story on domicide and home loss in Yarmouk Camp, Box 2.2). In a video they released online, Thomson joins Rania, a single mother, who wants to check the situation of her home. She has not been able to visit her home for five years as she fled the siege of the camp (Channel 4 News 2018). The video shows people searching for what remains of their belongings inside their homes. Without access to any form of transportation, all of them walked among the ruins while carrying their suitcases. One man found only a photo of his home. The journalist reported that soldiers were 'removing' people's belongings. However, the Channel 4 team was not permitted to film them, and they were told by their escort soldier that these soldiers were 'protecting' the valuables of the people. Most probably they were looting people's homes as soldiers and militia have done in different parts of Syria.

FIGURE 2.3 A woman and a child walking in the Old City of Homs, 2014.
Source: Omama Zankawan, taken by S.Z.

Rania, the single mother, walks between the ruins and sings whilst searching for her home. It is the hope and the dream that she will eventually be able to return home. The road to her home was blocked by debris, so she had to take another route. 'There is no home,' she weeps suddenly, pointing to a pile of rubble where her home once was. She stands in front of a collapsed building, determined to climb onto the ruins, weeping, pointing at her home, at her neighbourhood. The hopes of being able to return home are all gone. She squats on the ruins, weeping and then stands up, saying, 'Oh God, Oh God.'

FIGURE 2.4 Omama in her grandparents' flat in Homs, 2014.
Source: Omama Zankawan, taken by S.Z.

> **BOX 2.2 Hanan's story of displacement and domicide, 2021.**
>
> Almost ten years since I last slept in my own room back home. Yarmouk Camp, a Palestinian refugee camp in Damascus. Yarmouk was targeted with an airstrike followed by massive evacuation in 2012. Yarmouk was a safe haven for displaced people from neighbouring areas. As a punishment, Yarmouk was turned into a ghost town with only a few thousands living under inhuman conditions for years. People in Yarmouk lived under attacks of the regime and suffered from starvation.

Ten years away from home with a very thin chance of me ever going back. I still remember the last day in Yarmouk as if it was yesterday, I went early to work, in the city centre of Damascus, just two hours later I read the news that my neighbourhood was bombed. I was out and I could not go back ever since.

In 2018, under what the Syrian regime called 'a war on terror' our house was totally burned, we were told by people who lived in Yarmouk, that after the bombardment they deliberately burned the houses that were not affected much by the shelling and rockets. A friend of ours sent us photos and a video of our street and house after the end of the aggression. It totally broke my heart not to recognize my street from the first look. I had to see the pictures once, twice, and repeat to understand that this is the place I lived in, that under the rubble is what I still, to this moment, call home. Still, I could not link my memories to the pictures I saw. We had a small but a very bright apartment, with many windows. The kitchen was the second biggest room. It was the place where we spent our days, gathering around our wooden dining table, watching my mom cook or my little sister bake cake. It was all gone in the photos I saw later; the bright well-lit rooms were all eaten by the fire. It was also obvious, that our house was robbed before it was set on fire. The only things I recognized were the remains of the fridge and the bench of the dining table.

I left Syria in search of a good future and a safe place. Like many Syrians, I once dreamt of having freedom in Syria but ended up pursuing it abroad. Still, I hold home with me wherever I go. The news, the thoughts and the memories are part of my daily life. As much as I wish I could go back, I am afraid of facing the reality that what I have in mind is just an illusion, it is a memory and will forever be so. Many of our neighbours have also left Syria, others lost their lives under the attack of the regime. It is hard to think that they are not going to be around. See, it is not only about our house itself, but also about the small garden we had in the entrance of our building. It is about the small tailor shop on the ground floor, it is the teachers who used to give private lessons to students, and you would see the street full of their noise and laughter. It is about the small steps by the entrance door, where my sister used to sit with her friends after school. It is about me opening the window to say good morning to our neighbour.

I am a third-generation Palestinian refugee, my grandparents endured the loss of home and have lived the tragedy of exodus and refuge. They and my parents have worked for years to build a home away from home, and always had Palestine and the return in their minds and hearts. The tragedy we are enduring today goes even beyond, we are now mourning Palestine, Yarmouk and Syria, as if we inherited refuge, loss and exodus.

It is all gone. The place I call home is no longer the same and even if it was restored to its original status, who could restore the lost lives and the ones who escaped the country to save their lives?

As the famous Palestinian poet Mahmoud Darwish said:

> If they give you back the roads, who will give you back your steps? If they give you back your voice, who will give you back your words? And if they give you back the old cafes, who will give you back your friends?
> Hanan, a Syrian Palestinian architect based in Berlin

Domicide, and the multiple displacements that follow, cause both social disruption and personal trauma (Fried 1970). The repeated and unexpected displacements have a profound impact on the victims of domicide. The loss of home is not limited to physical loss, but also occurs in the emotional attachment to space where one feels they belong. This is what some scholars coin as 'un-homing' (Elliott-Cooper, Hubbard and Lees 2020), where displacement ruptures the connection between people and place with violence that causes negative emotional, psychological and material impacts. When I spoke to Jawad, who lost his family home, he told me how he feels rootless, although he still resides in his own city. His family eventually decided to sell the property and rent somewhere else in the city as the entire building was destroyed, and there was no reconstruction project for rebuilding their home.

In my conversation with Jawad, he told me how people feel like strangers in the city, not only those who have been displaced and those who lost their homes, but also those who remain where they are because the people and places around them have changed. He told me this is one of the main reasons why many people feel like strangers in their own cities as the people they cherish and the familiar friends and neighbours are no longer there.

Whilst we often hear about the number of displaced people and the number of destroyed buildings, we hear little about the impact of domicide on people. Scholars have investigated the impact of displacement and destruction on local communities. For instance, Rowland Atkinson has written about losing one's place, with a focus on the impact of gentrification in Australia. He brings together the loss of home with the complex feelings of alienation and argues that displacement entails feelings of displacement combined with a deeper set of social and psychological transformation. He also adds that even those who remain in their own place might endure a sense of alienation when neighbourhoods experience radical changes:

> displacement is comprised of more than simple 'boundary crossings' by households moving between neighbourhoods and out-migrating from gentrified areas. Such a perspective also forces us to consider why and how we might include those who remain in a neighbourhood as displacement because they endure experiences of alienation and newfound

disconnection from their neighbourhoods as the character of such places change. (Atkinson 2015: 377)

Responses to destruction

Several years after the end of the battlefields in Homs, most of the destroyed neighbourhoods in the city remain in ruins. Zankawan's own home remains destroyed, and her family is still unable to return to it. Until now, there are no reconstruction projects in Syria, leaving millions of people in a constant search for shelter. Despite the debates on reconstruction in the past few years (I will discuss reconstruction in more detail in Chapter 5), most of the responses to destruction in Syria have been limited to the rehabilitation of partially damaged buildings and infrastructure projects across different parts of the country (Al Masri 2013; Azzouz 2019). The work on rehabilitation has been carried out by different parties, including governmental institutions and local and international charities and NGOs. With the sanctions on Syria, the absence of political transition and the continuation of the conflict across different parts of the country, very few international organizations have worked from within the country, opening their offices mainly in Damascus, with other smaller branches in other cities. Some of the international organizations that have worked inside Syria are the Adventist Development and Relief Agency (ADRA), United Nations High Commissioner for Refugees (UNHCR), United Nations Development Programme (UNDP), the United Nations Children's Fund (UNICEF), Danish Refugee Council (DRC), the Norwegian Refugee Council (NRC) and the International Organization for Migration (IOM). The work of these organizations has varied in scope, focus and scale, and they have often worked with local charities on projects that respond to destruction and displacement.

Local charities have been active in supporting people in their struggle to find shelter and to respond to the radical changes in Homs. Whilst some of these charities have been established since before 2011, many have emerged in the past decade in response to the radical changes in living conditions in Homs. Today, there are more than 90 local charities in Homs. One of the best-known and very active charities is Jamiat Al-Bir wa Al-Khadamat Al-Ejtemaeia (Charity of Righteousness and Social Services). Al-Bir charity, as it is known, has undertaken significant work to rehabilitate partially damaged houses and to support internally displaced people to return to their homes (Pullan and Azzouz 2019). The charity was first established in 1956, ten years after Syria's independence in 1946 at the end of the French Mandate. With time, the charity has built up a strong name in Homs, and has established several projects that support marginalized communities such as an institute for blind people in 1959, a care home for the elderly in 1960 and a handicrafts centre for supporting women in need in 1962. As the types of projects have evolved and changed since its establishment, the charity has broadened its focus since 2011. For over a decade now, the charity has worked with youths who volunteer for social, cultural and educational projects. They have initiatives that encourage people to read, such as 'Read My Book'. In addition, the charity has an engineering office that looks at different aspects of the built environment. In collaboration with some of the INGOs (such as Oxfam, UNDP and UNICEF), Al-Bir Charity worked on the rehabilitation of the returnee's homes during 2015–18, helping thousands of IDPs to return to their partially damaged homes.

Several local charities, such as Al-Bir, have worked on the rehabilitation of partially damaged homes. People who had their homes destroyed have been invited to register their names with charities. These charities would then visit each of the registered families and assess their needs and situation. Based on this needs assessment, the charity would decide on how much repair they would offer. Depending on the situation of the family, their income and the number of family members, the charity would decide on how many rooms to rehabilitate in the flat. The priority is to enable people to return to their homes, even if parts of them are not rehabilitated, as long as these ruined homes are closed to the outside environment. In other cases, the charities have distributed shelter kits for people to repair and fix their own flats, with very basic materials such as plastic sheets, nails and wood frames. See-through plastic film has been given to close windows and plastic sheeting has been used as replacements for walls when families divide up flats into different spaces.

When I spoke with Abdallah in 2017, he told me that he volunteers in one of the local charities in Homs. One of the charity's teams visits families in need. He was assigned to Al-Iddikhar neighbourhood, which used to be a very quiet part of Homs but became crowded with IDPs. The team assigned for this neighbourhood included fifteen volunteers who visit IDPs, spending around twenty minutes with each of them to listen to their story before they make other visits. As part of his tasks, Abdallah visited single mothers, women whose husbands were killed, arrested or disappeared. He visited more than forty women, each of which has her own story of struggle and loss. Abdallah recalled one of these visits to a family who lived on the ninth floor in a tower block. There was no lift and it was extremely hot in the summer. When he walked up the stairs, he did not find the single mother. Her children told him that she worked as a labourer filling rice bags. He and his team entered the flat which was completely empty. There was only one small mattress for the family to sit on, a family of five children and their mother. The children's clothes were dirty and worn out, they looked miserable, and it seemed as if they had never had a shower in their life, he said. They looked hungry, and when they entered the kitchen, it was also empty. There was nothing but bread. 'It burnt my heart,' Abdallah spoke to me about the misery of the families they visited. He also spoke to me about the privilege and the power other families have in the same city, making it feel as if there were two separate universes inside Homs. The struggle of these women and their stories are often unheard, and the capacity of charities to support them is also limited. Abdallah told me that there are mothers who need so much help that it is far more than what the charity is able to offer. The charity can offer little support to these women due to the limited resources and the harsh conditions in which they live. How much he wished to do more, to provide more support, but he could not.

Responses of charities have been challenging due to the scale of the catastrophe in Syria: the mass destruction of the built environment and the displacement of millions of people. Their capacity to help in the rehabilitation has been especially limited due to a lack of funds, the collapse of the economy and the displacement of the workforce. A Homsi architect who worked for one of the charities spoke to me from his exile in Dubai. He told me about the dire situation in Homs, and how much more work is needed to support people. He noted that everything done by local and international charities and organizations represents '1%' of the actual work that should be done. The charities are working hard, he told me, they are trying to help families leave their collective shelters so they can return to their rehabilitated homes, but the capacity of these charities has been limited in the face of mass destruction. The work that these charities do is also dependent on the funds they get. And although many of them are collaborating and getting funds from other international organizations, these funds have stopped for many since 2017.

Charities as a collective act of solidarity

The impact of charities has moved beyond the help provided to the people they are serving. These charities have left a positive impact on the people who volunteered for them. Throughout their projects and wide range of initiatives, these charities attracted the youth at a time of chaos and unsettlement. Several people I spoke with explained how good they feel because they can contribute to the recovery of their own city, how they feel their voice matters, how they feel a sense of meaning and purpose. One of the young architects I spoke with told me that she feels her team at the charity is like a family for her as most of her friends and relatives have left Homs. Another architect told me he feels the positivity of the people he works with, and through this work at the charity he was able to cope with life in the midst of war. Amro, an architect who worked in one of these charities, explained his personal motivation for being part of the rehabilitation project.

He told me that the working conditions were hard in a city of ruins with the limited resources they had. However, all of this hard work was forgotten when they saw the happiness of a family they helped to get their home rehabilitated. He said some of the families they supported lived in collective shelters in schools, one of them even on the staircase of a school. But with the support of the city, they were able to rehome these families in need. This sense of solidarity, care and support for one another is what kept him working for the charity, until he eventually fled to Türkiye.

Zankawan spoke to me about the importance of the work of grassroot initiatives and the work that is carried out by local charities. Even with little resources and small-scale projects, they were able to bring a change to the city during the darkest times. One of these projects was painting some of the walls in Homs, which was seen as a radical transformation of the city by bringing colour to the ruins. As Zankawan told me (London, 2019):

> I remember one area in particular where people wanted to come back. And because it was all grey from destruction, some charities coloured all of the walls. They wrote 'coming back, we are back, we are back'. They drew a lot of trees. A lot of green, red, pink colours were on all the walls. I went there and just took photos of the walls because it was something beautiful in the middle of all the grey. I think they wanted people to feel the colours again maybe. Because I don't know why everything was just too grey. And it was a very nice initiative. It was very simple, just colour the walls, but people were happy. People were coming from all over Homs just to take photos and to see that area. It was very, very nice. I think they repeated that in a couple of other areas where people could go back to.

At the time of disconnection between architects and local communities, local NGOs have offered an alternative platform; a platform that already existed prior to 2011, but was not as active, visible and seen by young architects as in the past decade. Local NGOs brought architects closer to the struggles of the people, and initiated projects that require talking to impacted families and listening to their stories. At the time of despair and chaos, grassroot urban practices have emerged. People have been part of reclaiming their own urban space and shaping their own built environment. Local charities worked with communities and artists to paint murals on streets, and young men and women have removed the rubble from their streets. Documenting these efforts is essential as they celebrate the local resilience and make the local responses to destruction and displacement visible. Understanding these initiatives would also be essential for future reconstruction projects. Local charities could play a key role in reconstructing Syria as they have well-established engagement with local communities.

Architects at the time of war

Beyond local and international charities and organizations, the questions of destruction and displacement have been at the heart of the work of local architects, urban planners, activists, historians, academics and students. In my conversations with architecture students, many of them reported that their graduation project focused on the reconstruction and rehabilitation of a certain part of Homs. Despite the interest in writing and working on the questions of destruction and reconstruction by university students, many have told me that some of their academics have discouraged them from working on these themes, and would rather they worked on other types of projects that have nothing to do with the war.

One of the writers from inside Homs whose work has attracted international attention is Marwa Al-Sabouni. Her work has been shared widely through coverage in news media articles (e.g. in the *Guardian*, the *Financial Times*, CNN and BBC), and presentations at events and conferences in different cities across the world. Writing from Homs, Al-Sabouni published two books in the past decade, *The Battle for Home: Memoir of a Syrian Architect* (2016) and *Building for Hope: Towards an Architecture of Belonging* (2021). More than other cities, Homs has been centred in news headlines and reached into new academic circles globally. In her first book, she explains how the rehabilitation by the government is one-sided. She notes that the government removed the rubble and provided infrastructure for most parts of the Christian villages and districts in Al-Husn town, next to Krak des Chevaliers. For her, this one-sided support reflects the government's approach to punish Sunni communities for their anti-government stance. Sunni communities in these areas were left without support and were subject to arrest. She further explains that Sunni residents were prohibited from returning to live even in the ruins of their homes or were met with obstacles and mysterious incidents of abduction. She paints a picture of the living conditions there. Sunni communities who lost everything were sealing their windows with cardboard and scrappy pieces of wood to cover over the shell holes, whilst watching from their destroyed homes with eyes wide open the support given to their 'neighbours'.

Al-Sabouni's work has been widely circulated and referenced in the emerging debates on destruction and reconstruction in Syria. She was one of the earliest Syrian writers who published about the relationship between architecture and sectarianism, a topic that is rarely discussed in the architecture debates in Homs. Her first book, published in 2016, is one of the earliest cohesive works on post-2011 Homs, providing a courageous and brave voice from someone who is living inside a city of ruin and destruction. Her writing has influenced several architects both inside and outside Syria.

Young Syrian architects in Homs have been working on different projects and initiatives to respond to the destruction and displacement of their city. From assessing the damage to interviewing impacted families, from rehabilitating partially damaged homes to organizing walking tours in the Old City, these projects have been filled with passion, enthusiasm and a sense of pride. These architects are the ones who will build our Syria in the future. Every architect I spoke with has dreams and aspirations to shape the present and the future of Homs. Every one of them wants to see a better city, a better Homs. These dreams and aspirations, however, are challenged by the current difficult living conditions. There are limited opportunities to work on projects related to the built environment due to the lack of funds and limited resources. This makes it very difficult to establish any initiative or project independently. Furthermore, work that has been undertaken by local charities to rehabilitate partially damaged homes has decreased significantly since 2017 due to a lack of funds. Young architects struggle to find working opportunities in architecture, especially with the absence of any meaningful reconstruction project. Whilst still keen to work in architecture, many had no choice but to leave the country. Others remain in Homs but shift their career towards any opportunity that would offer some money to be able to afford living in Homs.

It is a tragic loss that these architects in Homs have no opportunity to shape the future of Homs. They expressed to me how excluded they feel by elderly and senior academics who are working on several reconstruction visions for Homs. They also feel that their voices are unheard in the increasingly growing number of events and seminars on Syria's reconstruction outside Syria. These young architects have the knowledge and the skills, and they have great ideas and creative visions for the future reconstruction. How great it would be if their visions are documented, and if their efforts to rebuild their cities are supported and enabled. When I spoke with one of these architects who works for an international organization in Syria, he stressed the importance of community engagement throughout the reconstruction processes. This is something that is missing in many conversations on reconstruction. Omar, who is in his early thirties, told me that the ideal scenario for the reconstruction is to keep people at the heart of it. He suggested building temporary homes for affected local families who would live in these homes whilst rebuilding their own ruined homes. In this way, he told me, internally displaced families contribute to the reconstruction of their own neighbourhoods and are partners with reconstruction companies. How could the efforts of these architects be supported? And how to create a safe space for them to come together and think individually and collectively about the future of Homs?

The university should be a platform to enable such initiatives and to foster free thinking. It should be the place for these creative ideas to be realized, and for young architects to suggest their post-war reconstruction ideas. The university should also be the place to learn about other cities that went through conflict and wars, and observe the challenges, mistakes and struggles when rebuilding them. Until now, there is little knowledge created at the university level about the destruction and reconstruction of the built environment in Syria. One exception is found at the International University for Science and Technology (IUST), where a reconstruction course was developed (IUST is 35 km from the centre of Damascus). The programme includes a historical review of several contested cities and how they were rebuilt in the aftermath of war. Then it moves to focus on the Syrian context, taking Homs as the focus. Part of the programme includes a visit to Homs where students and their supervisors visit different sites in the Old City. Students then return to their university and start working in groups. Local universities and academics should have a moral responsibility to focus on the reality of their own towns and cities, rather than teaching students how to design utopian projects disconnected from the current conditions in Syria.

'Everyone is an architect'

With the displacement of local architects, engineers and construction workers, the collapse of the economy and the struggle of charities to respond to the needs of impacted people, many Homsis have been left with one solution: to repair their ruined homes themselves. This self-repair is vital for many families to avoid the rising rental prices, as well as for their desire to return to their homes. Saleem, an architect in his early thirties, told me that he started taking some training courses through a local charity that helps people helping themselves. He told me he has been displaced nine times inside Syria since 2011, and he wanted to do whatever he could to make his family return to their home. When Saleem's family were first displaced, they moved to their relatives' home. They had one room for them, where the family of seven members lived. After living there for over six months, the family split in two different relatives' homes in the process of waiting to return to their home. Living with their relatives was a way to avoid paying rent that they could not have afforded after their income loss. Saleem then knew that their building was looted, burnt and destroyed. They registered with one of the local charities that was supporting families to repair their partially damaged homes. The waiting list was long, and it would take at least a year to get minimal support. Saleem started to repair the flat himself. One of his siblings was arrested, and his elderly father struggles to walk. He went each day to remove the rubble, spending hours and hours cleaning each room. He joined a metalsmith workshop so that he was able to repair whatever he could by himself with the support of construction workers whom his family hired. He told me how much he tried to make a temporary home in each place he moved to. His ultimate goal, however, was to repair his home so that his family can reunite. He kept going to his ruined home to repair it. In July 2019, he sent me a message saying that his mission had ended, that their home was repaired. He sent me a photo of a small car with a few bags and a mattress on top of it. They were returning home. Everything they ever owned was on top of that small car. Their home was looted.

One of the architects I spoke with and who works for an international NGO in Syria was complaining that 'everyone is an architect'. He was referring to the people who are taking the lead to repair their damaged homes and ruined shops. He was also referring to all the informal new constructions that have been made to expand properties and create extensions. These people are the 'architects' in Homs. When they felt abandoned and neglected. When they had to live in overcrowded rooms as the government was not giving them any form of support. They removed the rubble, cleaned the streets from debris, rehabilitated their own homes and designed their interior spaces. What is the alternative for them? This complaining architect did not acknowledge the struggle and the pain of these people, as if they had to wait for years to be able to access their ruined homes.

This is why many architects feel that they failed. They failed to support people when they needed help. They failed to engage with the people and understand their needs and wants. This sense of failure that some architects expressed to me was not only shaped by the post-2011 struggles, but also by the lack of engagement with communities before the war. Even today, many architects are working on luxury apartment projects (as we will see in Chapter 5), instead of working on social housing projects. The gap between architects and communities was extremely wide before 2011, and it has widened even more after the war. At the school of architecture in Homs, even today, many students are encouraged to focus their time and energy on utopian projects and tourist villages, rather than on responding to the massive scale of destruction. How can all of this change? What new ways of learning and thinking are needed today?

Conclusions

We rarely hear about the struggle of IDPs. Most of the conversations that have emerged about displacement of Syrians have been focused on those who cross the Syrian borders to countries such as Germany, Türkiye and Lebanon (Loveless 2013; Ostrand 2015; Baban, Ilcan and Rygiel 2017). We rarely hear about the work of how these local charities function with limited resources and in extremely difficult living conditions to support the most vulnerable, the ones who are searching for shelter inside Homs, like the work of Abdallah and his team. Furthermore, the story of IDPs is still largely untold.

Writing from inside Homs is extremely rare. Fear still prohibits people from publishing or sharing their thoughts publicly. Our understanding of what is happening inside Homs is limited due to the absence of free journalism and the lack of freedom in academia and beyond. In this chapter, I attempted to bring the stories of IDPs to the heart of the conversation about home. I relied on interviews with people who remain in Homs, or on those who left the city recently.

The past decade has been that of Syrian displacement. Many people I spoke with have been displaced several times. Neighbourhoods that were relatively safe suddenly became a battlefield, and hence, people again had to flee to another area. Many IDPs have established new lives in their new areas. They might have registered their children in schools, or moved them across universities – say, from Homs to Damascus University – and started getting the basic needs to make a living or find work. But again, this all changed when fighting escalated in the areas they moved to, causing another wave of forced displacement. Zankawan's family who rented another house and began making a new start had the second home they moved to destroyed.

What does it mean to lose home? I asked at the start of this book, and I asked the people I spoke with. It is not only the loss of the physical architecture, but a sense of disorientation when the people around us keep moving, and when the sense of community and neighbourhood gets destroyed. Speaking about home and writing about it is difficult. As Sarover Zaidi notes (2020), 'writing about homes is difficult, because it is writing about our families, our feelings and our fears. It is also writing about bodies, blankets, beds and beloveds, and how we learn to inhabit each of these, carry some along and also leave behind some.' It has been difficult for me to write about loss of home, and it has been difficult for the people I spoke with to talk about their home loss, but as Zankawan told me when I invited her to speak at a public event in London in 2019:

> This is the first time I talk about my story publicly. But I decided to come here after Ammar interviewed me a few months ago and I thought about it. I thought why haven't I talked about it before? And I really thought about it very much. I thought that this loss cannot be compared to other losses, to people who lost their lives, or mothers who lost their families. And then I realized again that: why do we put a size to a tragedy? It is all a tragedy. We can't see that this tragedy doesn't matter compared to another. So, that is why I decided to come here, to say that in reports and articles we read that thousands of buildings have been destroyed, are on the ground, but

we don't think of the memories that people have in these houses, the photos that we forgot. Honestly, until this moment, I still imagine myself putting that photo album, and trying to remember that I should pick it up. I didn't. So, this memory that is stuck with me is also stuck with millions of people. We need to humanize the numbers, to think that behind these destructions, there are people's memory, maybe some of them can build other memories, but other people maybe can't. And that's it.

3

Domicide and representation

Syria in exile

More than half of the Syrian population has been displaced from their homes. Across the world, two-thirds of the refugees come from only five countries, and at the top of the list is Syria, followed by Venezuela, Afghanistan, South Sudan and Myanmar. Those who fled Syria have found refuge across the world, mainly in neighbouring countries like Lebanon, Türkiye and Jordan, and beyond such as Egypt, Sudan, Germany and Sweden. Now, after more than a decade of displacement, millions of Syrian refugees and migrants are still unable to return, fearing for their own lives. Whilst we have found a refuge in the comfort of cities across the world, many of us still ache and yearn for our former homes.

From afar, memory of home floods back to the mind. In her book *The Future of Nostalgia*, Svetlana Boym (2001) notes that when we are at home, we do not need to talk about it. And being at home, for her, does not depend on an actual location, but rather it is a state of mind when things are in their right place, and so are we. For the millions of refugees across the world, home is talked about as many live with a tremendous sense of injury, with a sense of rootlessness and homelessness, where things are not in their right place. The main feature of exile, according to Boym, is its double consciousness. For those who are away from the places they grew up in, life abroad might feel like being divided into two, one in exile and the other in the place they left. Many of us who have escaped the horrors of war and live in the comfort of cities such as London, Berlin, Cairo and Istanbul still feel as if we left Syria but Syria never left us. From afar, we see our country crumbling into ruins, and we see people drowning in the sea, we see our former neighbours pushed into forced displacement and extreme poverty, and we feel the pain of being away from the people we love who are suffering each day, even to get their daily bread.

Many of the Syrian refugees and migrants I met are building a new home in their exile, but once I start the conversation with them, I witness the deep suffering and the levels of trauma, loss and grief each of them has been experiencing, even thousands of miles away from the bloodshed in Syria. Arriving on the shores of new safe lands is by no means the end of the struggle of those escaping violent environments. Displacement is not only about the annihilation of physical buildings but is also about the disruption of interpersonal networks and the destruction of different aspects of identity (Zhang 2018). A study that builds on interviews with 11,452 Syrians between 2008 and 2015 found that Syrians were five times less likely to report having someone to count on after the start of the conflict (Cheung et al. 2020). Due to the displacement of over half of the population, millions of us have found ourselves separated from our families and friends, from the networks of support, solidarity and friendships that we built up before 2011. The study also shows that hope, life satisfaction, feeling respected, freedom in life and social support, have all dropped since 2011. Positive emotions dropped from 70 per cent in 2008 to less than 40 per cent in 2014. Domicide should not only be thought of as the destruction of the physical home, but also as the human suffering and the living experiences of the making and unmaking of homes.

When our present is filled with uncertainty, chaos and loss, we tend to look at our past home as if it is a place of security, identity, sanctuary and tranquillity. Many of the Syrians I met and interviewed in the past few years deal with this tension between the past and the present, between home and exile. It is the doubleness that Boym talks about in her work. When refugees look back at their former home from their new home countries, they look at themselves in the past, they look at their former lives. This doubleness of exile and the exposure of different times and places has been powerfully and emotionally depicted by Iranian artist Shirin Neshat. In her video *Soliloquy* (1999), Neshat explores themes of exile, identity and cultural history. She places the viewer in between two screens which face each other. One screen shows Neshat in Mardin in Türkiye. There is a sense of calmness, peace, quietness as some of the scenes take place inside a courtyard building with a fountain at the heart of it. Children are playing and swimming. She walks calmly, touching the leaves of a tree in the courtyard. The other screen shows Neshat in the city in which she currently resides, New York. The scenes in New York show the fast pace of life, the crowded underground stations, the people rushing around her. I watched this film at Tate Modern in London in 2021. As a viewer, I experience this sense of in-betweenness, sitting on the threshold of two worlds. But it is not only the viewer watching these two different scenes; Nishat is, too. She looks at herself. When she is walking in the left-hand screen in New York, she would pose on the right-hand screen in Mardin to look at and observe herself. She does the same when posing in Mardin to look at herself in New York. Neshat's work has been shaped by her own experiences of exile. When she was seventeen, she left Iran for the US to complete her education, but whilst there the Islamic Revolution broke out in 1979 preventing her from returning home. She was only able to return and visit nearly two decades after she left. She notes that *Soliloquy* is based on her own experiences of living in the state of 'in-between' and highlights the advantages and disadvantages of this in-betweenness. The advantages for her are the exploration of new cultures and the freedoms of living in the US, whilst the disadvantages are the inability of being the 'centre' or at 'home' anywhere (Tate Modern 2021). Whilst art has been a medium to tell the story of exile and displacement, I hope in the current chapter to use this lens to understand the different representations of domicide in the Syrian context.

In Lebanon, Jordan, Sudan, Egypt, Türkiye, Germany, Sudan, the US and many other countries, Syrians see their broken country crumbling in ruins from afar. Like Neshat, they look from their exile at their past lives, to the places that they can no longer visit, to places that no longer exist, to the memory of people who may or may not be alive any more. In exile, the lost objects, places and spaces are remembered, reimagined and reconstructed. People of my city, Homs, who live in the UK, Switzerland and France decorate the interior of their homes with drawings, paintings and photographs of Homs as can be seen in Figure 3.1(*a*). Some of them who migrated before the revolution have even brought Syrian-made furniture for their homes. One of the most featured landmarks in Homs is the New Clock Tower, which I highlighted in Chapter 2. Not only Homsis reflect on this site as a way to remember a pre-war life in the city, but also to reflect on the Revolution as the New Clock Tower has turned into a revolutionary symbol and a site where people gathered to protest. The New Clock Tower's symbolism of the city, its past and its recent struggle, has led many Syrians to reconstruct it inside Syria when they were protesting in other cities and towns as well as in other parts of Homs when the site was besieged by the regime. But what I found so emotional is that the Clock Tower was also reconstructed in a refugee camp in Greece. Figure 3.1(*b*) shows the Clock Tower reconstructed with a sign stating: '19.03.2016. 23:15. Life stopped after we entered Katsikas camp.' Was it an attempt to reconstruct a home in this temporary refugee camp? Was it an ache to Homs? Was it a way to recapture a lost world by reconstructing a memory of their former home?

In refugee camps, in homes and cities around the world, another Syria is reconstructed in exile. When visiting Syrian restaurants in cities such as Berlin, London, Manchester and Beirut, I feel like I was back in Syria. Once you open the door and enter, you feel as if you are in Syria. Everyone is speaking Arabic with diverse Syrian dialects, perhaps you may recognize some of the familiar faces or friends from the Syrian communities – this happens to me when I visit restaurants in London where I reside or in

FIGURE 3.1(a) Homs Clock Tower at Homsi House in London, 2021.
Source: Sana Kikhia.

Figure 3.1(b) A replica of the New Clock Tower in a refugee camp in Greece, 2016.
Source: Katie Wong.

Manchester when I visit. Fairuz songs are being played, reminding us of an older rhythm of life, of times that we can no longer reclaim or capture, as if these songs are taking us back to another, former life. Back in Syria, many cafes, restaurants, buses and taxis would play Fairuz songs daily. In these restaurants, the decorations and furniture are familiar. Paintings and drawings of homes, streets and monuments in Syria are hanging on the walls. Photographs of Syrian writers, activists, artists and intellectuals are featured. But above all, it is the smell that brings the memory like a flood of lost times, of lost people, of lost events bringing us closer to our former selves.

For those who are forcibly displaced from their homes, memory and identity are reconstructed and renegotiated daily. In *Places of Pain*, Hariz Halilovich (2013) writes about the new places of settlement of those who fled the 1992–5 war in Bosnia and Herzegovina. He notes that forced displacement radically reshapes identity that may lead to feelings of permanent misplacement. Even when arriving at the comfort of new home countries, diasporic communities, according to Halilovich, experience the complexity of the interplay between place, memory and identity. Halilovich notes that this complexity is more intense when the places which communities have left are scarred, vandalized, destroyed, divided up. These ruined places that turn into sites of suffering, trauma and humiliation are also the places of desire for the displaced survivors who wish to return even if only to visit these ruins.

I have found similar themes emerging in the Syrian context. From different corners across the globe, memory is being reconstructed, with efforts varying from living experiences in exile where the former life is rebuilt daily and slowly through food, language and culture to establishing platforms and projects to revive and preserve memory. But what memory can be brought to the conversation today? Which slices of history are brought to the consciousness of the Syrian diaspora? There is no doubt that when there is not much left of our past and its materiality, memory is used more and more to make sense of who we are and where we are heading.

During my research, I started asking people about memory and why memory is becoming more and more talked about in the Syrian context compared to pre-2011 times. Dawn Chatty, the author of *Syria: The Making and Unmaking of a Refuge State* (2018), explained to me the importance of memory for forcibly displaced people. Chatty, who has researched and published extensively on dispossession and displacement to and from the Levant, told me that those who are forcibly displaced might leave their countries having literally nothing with them. Yet, the memory of the people and the places they left remain with them. In her research, Chatty focused on the forced displacement towards Syria over the past 150 years, where people found refuge and sanctuary, including Circassians, Ashkenazi and Sephardic Jews, Armenians, Albanians, Kosovars, Palestinians, Lebanese and Iraqis.

Chatty told me that memory is not only important for those who have been forcibly displaced to recover their past, but also for imagining and shaping the future reconstruction of our ruined cities:

> Memories are extremely important. And the past is extremely important. When people are displaced or dispossessed, very often they lose everything they have; their homes might have been blown up, their quarters are destroyed. In order for them to be recreated, something to be put in a place that is comfortable for those who lived there, you have to depend upon memory or drawing or writing or photography. I know many people who experienced troubles, they kept their photographs in a safe place to help revive the memory. For architects, having the drawings means you can remember them, and you can celebrate them, but also reconstruct them. And this is extremely important, especially when you are dealing with a brutal state that is trying to create a different state. (Online interview, 2019)

I arrived at Chatty's work after reading her publications on Syria (2017, 2018). When borders were closing for Syrians and when we have been seen as a burden on host countries, I have found a sanctuary in Chatty's writing that contrasts with what one would see in the news. Through her research, she has reopened the history of Syria as a place that welcomed communities escaping persecution, violence and wars. This history is not known to many; a history of tolerance, openness and hospitality. Her work brought me back to my life in Homs. I remembered my Iraqi and Palestinian neighbours and friends, my Circassian schoolmates, my family's friends who left Lebanon for Homs. When there is a collective forgetting about multiculturalism in Syria, I always feel that we must fight to remember.

The nostalgia for a lost past and the yearning to return to revisit traces of history, to recapture our fading lives, have led to the explosion of cultural and artistic works that deal with the notion of memory by Syrians and their allies who responded to domicide. The year 2011, the turning page in the history of Syria, is also the mark for the birth of a memory boom. With the start of the Syrian Revolution, several initiatives inside and outside Syria have been established to collect photographs, films and oral history of cultural heritage and everyday life before and after 2011. I frame them in this chapter as the different representations of domicide through the lens of arts and culture.

With the emergence of arts and culture as a response to domicide, new platforms have also been established. At Rethink Rebuild Society, a Manchester-based charity (informally started in 2011 but formally registered as a charity in 2018), an annual festival, Celebrating Syria, has been organized since 2017. The festival provides a space for Syrian artists, writers, musicians, architects and filmmakers in the UK and beyond to share their cultural and artistic work. The festival attracts people who are interested in Syria's culture, including the Syrian diasporic communities, of whom many are unable to return to Syria. It is also important for those who are not from Syria to connect with the Syrian culture that moves beyond images of war. In 2022, another festival was launched, the Syrian Arts and Culture Festival (SACF), which is similar to Celebrating Syria, dedicated to showcasing the vibrant Syrian arts and culture to audiences in the UK. Both of these festivals have taken place in the UK across Manchester and London, respectively.

However, not only physical platforms have emerged to promote and centre Syrian voices but also online platforms have emerged to focus on everyday life before the war. Examples include Syria Before 2011, a project that collects photographs of everyday life before the war, mostly taken by travellers (Iskandarani 2019), and Qisetna (which means Our Story), that publishes stories of Syrians from different parts of the country, writing about their precious memories and cultural identity. These initiatives have brought with them an alternative narrative about Syria that contrasts with the images of Syria in the news media. As millions of displaced Syrians are no longer able to return to Syria, memory projects have become a way to fight to remember, to not forget. But this fight to remember is not only limited to the pre-2011 times; rather, many Syrians want to remember and preserve the memory of the post-2011 struggle so that their pain and sorrow are not erased.

Each year, significant moments of the Syrian Revolution are remembered and commemorated. The anniversary of the Syrian Revolution is remembered in March across different cities in the world. Thousands of Syrians march in streets of cities such as London, Manchester, Berlin and New York as a continuation of the struggle. The memory of the start of the revolution is kept alive with global events, protests, marches and presentations. Projects and initiatives have also been established in order to build an archive of the Syrian Revolution, such as the Creative Memory of the Syrian Revolution that currently has over 11,000 items linked to the map of Syria. The archive includes paintings, drawings, posters, murals and videos. Questions of memory and remembrance emerge today much more than the times before the revolution. It feels as if, suddenly, we rediscovered our past, and as the past is being erased, we want to fight domicide.

How to preserve the memory of pre- and post-2011? How to resist forgetting? Can the memory of the struggle be preserved spatially in the future of cities in Syria through museums, streets and squares names? These questions are already in the minds of some of the people I speak to. However, they acknowledge how memory is contested and narrated by those in political power. The regime is already building new war memorials and statues at the time of destruction and displacement, whilst those who lost their beloved ones for the revolution remain silent inside Syria (González Zarandona and Munawar 2020). These one-sided memorials, however, further divide people who have suffered so much in the last decade. At the time when people are already divided, this selective memorialization spatially segregates people and poses questions about who has the right to be remembered or kept forgotten in the city.

The memory of the struggle in the city often comes up in my conversations with Syrian architects, activists and writers. For them, memory should not only be preserved in archives, but also spatially in the city. Some have even suggested to me the need to preserve parts of the ruins of the war for future generations to remember the horrors we have been through. Approaches to remembering the times of violence vary across cities. But it is by no means new. After the atom bomb was dropped on Hiroshima in 1945, a surviving building, the Hiroshima Prefectural Industrial Promotional Hall (constructed in 1914) was kept standing in ruins. It was later renamed the Hiroshima Dome, and is now a UNESCO World Heritage Site. This was also the case in Coventry, a city in central England that was extensively bombed during the Second World War (Figure 3.2). In a competition that attracted tens of designs,

FIGURE 3.2 Coventry Cathedral, 1962.
Source: Arup.

the winning proposal kept the cathedral roofless instead of rebuilding it. Today, after nearly sixty years since its destruction, the cathedral remains as one of the most iconic symbols of the city's past and present. In Berlin, remnants of the Berlin Wall still stand in the landscape of the city, reminding Berliners and visitors of a divided past. In Beirut, a building that was constructed in 1924 on the former Green Line that divided Beirut during the Civil War of 1975–90 has been transformed into a museum, Beit Beirut. In France, Oradour-sur-Glane is one of the most remarkable examples of preserving the ruins of war. On 10 June 1944, over 642 men, women and children were shot or burnt alive, and the village was destroyed. After the war, it was decided to preserve the ruins as a place to remember the people who were massacred there. A survivor of the massacre who lost his mother and two sisters said that, 'it's always difficult for me to come here . . . I relive my village in my head, hear its old sounds, put faces to the ruins. But it's important to preserve these ruins and keep telling the story so that it can continue to be passed down when we're no longer here' (Chrisafis 2013). With the gradual disappearance of war ruins from cities that witnessed conflicts and destruction, many activists and architects campaign to preserve the dark history spatially. In *Ruin Lust*, the critic Brian Dillon (2014) asks, 'why are we fascinated by ruins?' He suggested that ruins (and not only those of war):

Recall the glory of dead civilisations and the certain end of our own. They stand as monuments to historic disasters, but also provoke dreams about futures born from destruction and decay. Ruins are bleak but alluring reminders of our vulnerable place in time and space.

There are attempts by those in political power to erase the memory of the war, and to pretend that nothing has happened. Under the shiny new buildings, the sorrows and miseries are buried. There are attempts to rewrite history, and to reshape the narrative so that the pain of the people is whitewashed, silenced, neglected and erased. The narrative in the Syrian context is already being redirected by political powers. The voices of the people are often overshadowed and marginalized. In my conversations with Chatty, she told me that (online interview, 2019):

There is a very clear government effort to rewrite Syria's contemporary population and maybe even to rewrite the past; nobody challenges it. The only way you could challenge this effort to re-write or to exclude is by your memory, by not forgetting and using all the tools that you have, even if it is out of place, because someday you can go back. I think the efforts to restore on paper at least the quarters of Homs that were destroyed, the quarters in Aleppo that were destroyed, are important for rebuilding. The government is planning to level these areas to put up something else.

Since 2011, two themes have been constructed on the struggle of Syria: displacement and destruction. The first theme has turned Syria into an image of displacement, with lines of displaced people crossing borders, taking dangerous sea journeys or living in refugee camps. These images have been cemented in the minds of people without any context or knowledge about Syria. However, the way in which displaced people have been portrayed is as if they were powerless, weak and without agency. In my conversation with Chatty, she told me that:

> The refugee regime, which is very European oriented, promotes an image of the refugee as a vulnerable, weak, passive individual who has lost everything and has to depend on the international system in order to survive. The international refugee regime applies this image to most of mass influxes of people from Uganda to Tanzania or Kenya or from Burma to Bangladesh, this image is cultivated. The big shock of the west was that the refugee image is being turned a little bit upside down. The image of the Iraqi refugees, for example, before the Syrian crises did not fit their picture, because those people who were able to flee Iraq were middle-class professionals. The image making as part of the UN agencies to raise funds and help refugees did not work out with Iraqi refugees and did not work well with Syrian refugees outside of the 2015 mass influx into Europe. If you are on the road for weeks and weeks walking and you have no chance to shower, no chance to eat, anybody will look unkept, and this was the image of 2015. But what has been ignored is that they have not lost everything. Even if they were unable to bring something with them, it does not mean that they are powerless, or have no agency. So, the image of the refugee is developed in order to create better fund raising opportunities but does not always fit the facts on the ground.

The second theme that has become synonymous with Syria is the image of destruction, with the mass destruction of villages, towns and cities in Syria. The representations of this destruction have varied. For instance, in London, a 3D replica of the Arch of Triumph in Palmyra, which was destroyed by ISIS in 2015, was exhibited at Trafalgar Square. Boris Johnson, who was mayor of London at the time, gave a speech on the opening day and wrote a couple of articles about Palmyra (Johnson 2016), and in one of them he said:

> We are here in the spirit of defiance . . . Defiance of the barbarians who destroyed the original of this arch and destroyed so many other monuments

and relics in Syria and in the Middle East and in Palmyra . . . Congratulations to the Institute of Digital Archaeology. How many digits do you think Daesh deserve? I think two digits to Daesh . . .

In Palmyra itself, a concert was held by Russian composers using the ancient heritage site, with its celebrity-like status, to send global messages to the world (*The Economist* 2016). Whilst much coverage has been directed towards cultural heritage sites, little has been told about the everyday spaces, and little has been told about the people, and little has been told by the people. The interest in the ancient, the monumental and the historic has also led to building an image about Syria as an ancient site, whilst little is done to look at the communities and the contemporary urban lives. How can we resist domicide? How can we resist the rewriting of history? I personally believe that art has been central in answering these questions. I believe that through arts and culture and through the work of artists, we can tell an alternative story about the Syrian struggle. This is why in the following sections I will focus on the work of Syrians and allies across the world who are pushing the boundaries to retell the story of Syria and Syrians. Through their work, they attempt to deal with diverse themes of memory, nostalgia, domicide and reconstruction.

Artists' responses to domicide

Images of domicide in Syria have been sweeping across the world. Syria has become synonymous with destruction, ruins and displacement. These images have reached out to a global audience, and many artists have attempted to understand what is happening in Syria and have responded to domicide. This has led to the emergence of a new wave of artistic efforts that deal with questions of exile, displacement, urban destruction, protests, identity and many other themes both by Syrians and international artists who have stood in solidarity with Syria and Syrians (Halasa, Omareen and Mahfoud 2014; Cusenza 2019). Syrian artists have found in their artwork a tool to preserve the memory of the country and a platform to shed light on the horrors of war. The work of these artists has been shaped by their own losses as many of them lost their homes and have been displaced. When I spoke to artist Tarek Touma, a former medical student who later studied fine art in London where he currently resides, he told me how his work changed after 2011. Red, abstraction and distortion are more dominant in his post-2011 work. In one of his paintings, Touma paints the destruction of his own hometown, Douma, just outside Damascus. Other artists who are not from Syria have responded to domicide, too. Artist Julie Mehretu, who was born in Addis Ababa, Ethiopia, in 1970 and currently lives and works in New York City, has produced a large-scale six-part print titled *Epigraph, Damascus*. The artwork includes drawings of buildings from Damascus with their structures drawn in fine lines. But these buildings are fading away or even invisible from a distance as layers and layers of print overlap one another, creating a sense of chaos, instability and violence.

Another artist whom I had the chance to interview for this research is Tiffany Chung, who now lives and works in Vietnam and the USA. Chung produced 40 maps on Syria as part of The Syria Project. She wanted to revisit and reopen historical questions in Syria's past as well as look at the post-2011 Revolution. In her maps, Chung wanted to respond to the Arab Spring, when millions of people were asking for their rights and freedoms. Her first map was of Homs. I asked why Homs, and she said because it is 'The Capital of the Revolution'. As I mentioned in Chapter 2, Homs got this nickname due to the consistent mass protests in the city when other parts of the country witnessed lesser protests at the time. In 2014, Chung worked on Homs in her map, *31 Days in the Capital of Revolution*. The map is based on tracking protests in Homs between 28 September and 28 October 2011 (Figure 3.3). In addition to the map of Homs, Chung worked on an installation titled,

FIGURE 3.3 *31 Days in the Capital of the Revolution*, 2014. Ink and oil on vellum and paper, 79 × 100 cm.

Source: Tiffany Chung.

finding one's shadow in ruins and rubble. As part of the installation, Chung wrote a poem on the theme of the return to places that have been erased and ruined:

> The city resurrects momentarily from its death,
> when the first sun ray hits its debris.
> Lovers walk around, hand in hand,
> before realizing they can't find their own shadows.
> Children ride bicycles up and down little hills
> they don't remember being there – eyes wide open before nightfall,
> before all disappear behind distorted walls
> and into dark bullet holes.

Chung's work on Syria is influenced by her experiences of loss and trauma. She lived through the Vietnam War and its aftermath. Her father was captured and imprisoned when she was eleven years old. It took her ten years to return to Vietnam after she fled as a child refugee. She told me (online interview, 2021):

> Tracking the ongoing conflict and displacement in Syria has brought me back to confronting the war in Vietnam and its aftermath. The more I collect data on Syria, the more I am reminded of Vietnam. Although these are two different contexts, the war in Syria gives me a lot of flashbacks. With such raw emotions, you can sympathize with others even when you don't fully know their pain.

In her work on Syria, she wanted to come closer to her own history, but also to get closer to the pain of others in Syria. Chung told me how she felt the urgency to work on The Syria Project as the world seems to forget Syria. She told me that dealing with one's own trauma takes time:

> It is important for me to delve into the history of Vietnam but it often takes time to process trauma. And it certainly took me time to deal with my own. But in the Syrian case, I felt there was an urgency to work on The Syria Project. With all the media-saturated images and information, we've become numb – people, especially refugees, have become just numbers in statistical data. What do we do when ongoing mass destruction and displacement fade away in global public consciousness together with hope? And in a world where there is too much of everything, what can I do as an artist to remind people that the crisis in Syria is still going on? The Syria Project helps me to confront my own history and through this project, I hope to continue to draw people's attention to Syria.

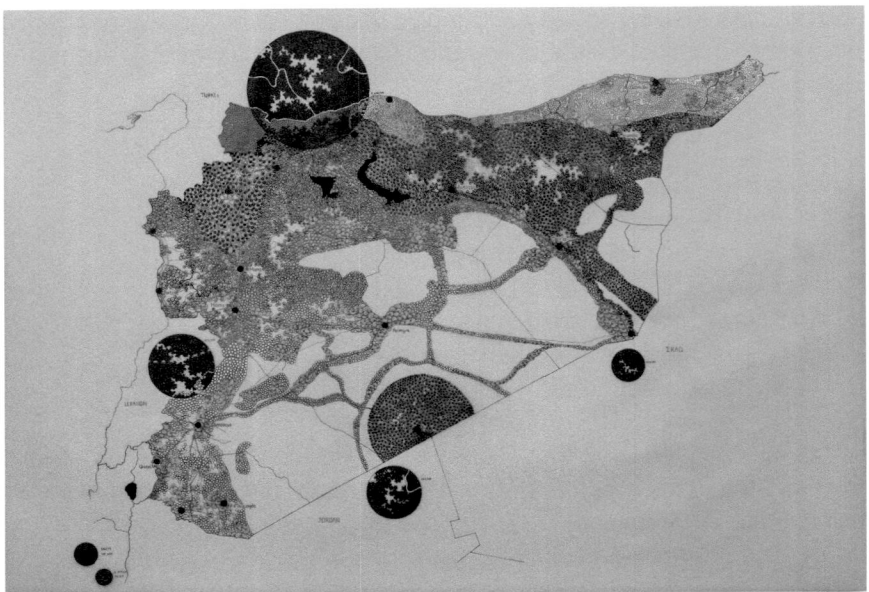

FIGURE 3.4 ISW: areas of control; UNHCR: numbers and locations of Syrian refugees and IDPs as of April 2019. Acrylic, ink and oil on vellum and paper, 76 × 93 cm.

Source: Tiffany Chung.

Chung used mapping as the main medium for The Syria Project (Figure 3.4). Mapping 'gives people a way to revisit and to recall certain memories'. She has worked with young Syrian refugees on map-making (2016–17), and she told me that the collective mapping created 'a safe space' to tell the story of Syria and Syrians. 'Mapping helps to flesh out your memories through focusing and reflecting, which is crucial for these youngsters to regain hope and direction in life. It's also important to reclaim the narrative with your own memories.'

Deanna Petherbridge: On domicide of Homs

Much has been done by artists to respond to domicide, but I have been particularly attracted to the work of one artist who spent months and months drawing the destruction of my city, Homs. Unlike the quick-and-fast cinematic moments of destruction that we watch on the news and with the flood of information on Syria, the work of artist Deanna Petherbridge invites the viewers to stop, to slow down, to think, to make sense of the loss.

Petherbridge's work is an act of homage to the people of Homs, to Homs. It is an eloquent condemnation of domicide. In her drawing, she goes beyond the fast consumption of images to zoom into the details of destruction, as if in between the lines she is telling the story of domicide, of the people who are no longer there – absent from the city and absent in the drawing. She explores Homs as an imagined site of trauma, a city of ruins and rubble, a city of displaced people who lost their homes. I arrived at Petherbridge's work when I visited Tate Britain in London in 2019. A giant drawing stretching over three panels got my attention from a distance. The ruins looked familiar even though there was no direct link to Homs: the creatureless and vegetationless buildings and streets, the falling roofs, the broken windows, all reminded me of Homs. I suspected it might be a drawing of Homs. So, I read the title and it was *The Destruction of the City of Homs*.

Petherbridge only knew of Homs through what she found in news reports, media articles and videos. But despite that, she told me, 'I have a moral obligation' to attempt to understand what this war means to people who lost their everyday lives. From afar, she drew the city of Homs; imagining the houses, the office buildings, the mosques and the everyday life in a contemporary modern city. She dealt with the drawing with a great sense of care, responsibility and an enormous amount of detail. Inside the empty ruined rooms and between the collapsed structures, frames and stones are piled on top of one another, of what was once the home, the office of someone. Whilst this drawing focused on the city of Homs and the ruins of everyday places and spaces (Figure 3.5), Petherbridge created another drawing of Syria in response to the destruction of the ancient cultural site of Palmyra as a metaphor to the destruction of history (Figure 3.6).

I explained to Petherbridge that, after years of struggle in Syria, the Syrian people are being turned into numbers in the news media and in international humanitarian reports. I told her how painful it feels that Syrians have become the news in a fast-moving world where viewers will watch our struggle and then continue doing what they are doing, I told her what it feels like to be forgotten, how our struggle is being erased. She told me (London, 2019):

> I feel the most terrible outrage that people can eat a meal in front of the television and watch the destruction of a city and be unmoved by it. We have all seen the ragged lines of migrants on our screens fleeing bombed homes and towns and of course, more recently, economic migrancy in South America. I can't watch these pictures. I can't watch the destruction of environments anywhere without having some attempt to understand what it means to people to lose their livelihoods, to lose their families, their identities.

FIGURE 3.5 *The Destruction of the City of Homs*, 2016. Ink and wash on paper, framed dimensions 127.7 × 252 × 5 cm.

Source: Deanna Petherbridge. Courtesy of the artist. Photographer: John Bodkin.

FIGURE 3.6 *The Destruction of Palmyra*, 2017. Ink wash on paper, triptych, framed dimensions (approx.) 145 × 369 cm.

Source: Deanna Petherbridge. Courtesy of the artist. Photographer: Stephen White.

You get frozen, I imagine as a refugee, you get frozen the moment you leave your home and your country. So, you enter a timeless as well as a spaceless kind of world, I imagine. And because we are now facing a world where everybody is on the move for different reasons the situation is too horrific. The problem as an artist is to think how I might deal with this. Do I have the right? Can I deal with such immense issues without being false, without being superficial?

All of these things were very, very much in my mind when I was doing the drawing. It took me months and months because I was working on it with such obsessive detail. For me the attention to detail was an act of homage to those so brutally displaced.

In my conversations with Petherbridge, I got closer to her work, to the concepts and ideas that she is dealing with in her drawings, with a wide range of themes such as borders, migration, war and violence. One of the themes that drew me to Petherbridge's work is the destruction of history. In our conversations, she has referred to her own neologism: Historophobia and, as she puts it, the fear of history. So that the fear of other people's history leads to the destruction of their history by those in power. The destruction of history in Syria, which has captured the news platforms, is not limited to the destruction of people's symbols, monuments, religious buildings and cultural heritage sites, but is also domicide, the targeting of people's way of living, the erasure of entire neighbourhoods to the ground. It is the destruction of home, and the destruction of the market, the evacuation of communities and the forced displacement of millions of people to create a 'healthier' society, that the Syrian regime once stated. Historophobia is the erasure of the physical and the built environment of the people, but it is also the fear of their intangible history, their traditions and cultures, their stories and memories, so that these people are kept silenced, marginalized and disempowered. It is also the attempt to whitewash the history of struggle and the destruction of the memory of resistance, so that those in power rewrite their own history whilst fearing the history of others.

Conclusions

Whilst millions of people have reached out to new lands having literally nothing with them, they reconstructed another home in their exile. This home in exile has been built and reconstructed through rituals, traditions, food, culture and art. As Syria becomes another forgotten war, a faceless war, synonymous with ruins and decay, how can we make sense of the trauma and loss that Syrians have endured, both individually and collectively? What story can be told about Syria? And how can it be narrated? Artists, writers, activists and scholars have been at the forefront to answer these questions. Since 2011, they have pushed the boundaries to tell another story about Syria: a story that is different from what we see presented by the news agencies; a story of rebellion, resistance and beauty. From writing and painting, to documenting and researching, their efforts are ways that help us fight to remember. Their work, however, remains scattered, disconnected and fragmented, with little research directed towards understanding the emerging wave of artistic work on post-2011 Syria – collectively. More future research is needed to explore the role of the arts in times of violence and war. Some of the questions that should be asked include: how have artists responded to domicide since the start of the Syrian Revolution in 2011? and how has the revolution enabled the emergence of new artistic works in exile, giving voices to those who have been disadvantaged and marginalized in the artistic circles?

In this chapter, I hope that I have contributed towards the emerging work of Syrian artists in exile who are preserving the memory of the revolution and engaging with different themes such as: the trauma of displacement, the practice of loss and the separation that millions of people are living by being away from the ones they love and the places they cherish. Outside Syria, there are great efforts to resist domicide, to resist the destruction of history. There are many Syrians and international allies and friends who are pushing in every possible way to tell the story of Syria, to carry on with the journey towards justice and freedom. I did not want to present the work of Syrians only, but also bring to the conversation the great work done by artists from outside Syria whose work shines light in the dark and brings a hopeful future of solidarity and empathy. The work of friends and allies who have stood in solidarity with Syrians and Syria has been essential to build these foundations. As Petherbridge told me (London, 2019):

> It is wonderful to see the story told by different people (not only Syrians) who contribute to documenting, archiving, narrating, researching Syria at the time of war; and these multiple contributions are extremely valuable. Art of course is at the forefront. Your work is one of these great contributions.

Syrians outside Syria have distance from the country, and might have the tools and resources to raise their words and to carry on with the struggle through their art. The story of Syria will continue to be told and retold by many people. From paintings, drawings, concerts and literature to films and exhibitions, artistic and cultural efforts have been essential in building foundations of solidarity across the world. Now, after more than a decade of war in Syria, art and culture are at the forefront to preserve memory. These efforts are some of the tools and devices that we must use to continue the struggle for justice and freedom in Syria, but they are also ways of dealing with the individual and collective trauma we have experienced as people even in the darkest times. As Sarah Fine put it, in times of crises, the arts are the weapons of the soul (Fine 2020).

4

Domicidal reconstruction

In *Reconstructing Spain: Cultural Heritage and Memory after Civil War*, Dacia Viejo-Rose (2014) explores the role of cultural heritage in the aftermath of the Spanish Civil War of 1936–9. Viejo-Rose explains how history and identity are remodelled through the physical destructions and reconstructions. Reconstruction, she argues, could emerge as the new landscape of contestation. Through a one-dimensional narrative and a one-sided approach to memory and memorialization, divisions between people are further cemented instead of bringing communities together. Viejo-Rose highlights how reconstruction at the time of dictatorship can be used as a propaganda device to smear the vanquished as the regime in power controls popular memory 'through its totalitarian grip on the media and the education system, on public memorials and commemorations as well as the monopoly of choices about what to preserve, rebuild or neglect'. Reconstruction can bring with it new destruction that erases the past in an attempt to create a place of forgetting, as in Gernika, in the autonomous Basque Country in northern Spain:

> Through the vehicle of reconstruction . . . in erasing traces of what had actually happened, in attempting to rewrite history and build a new Gernika, in trying to absorb the town's unique symbolism into a national ideology, the [Francoist] regime was consciously forging not a place of memory but a 'place of forgetting'. (Viejo-Rose 2011: 134)

Fears and anxieties surround the debates of reconstruction in Syria today, not only because reconstruction can be used to oppress, but also because it can create more loss and rupture in the name of creating a new world. In several war-torn cities, reconstruction is seen as an opportunity to 'modernize' the city and to 'rethink' it; a time to start from scratch and build a new image whilst forgetting the wartime period, and even in some extreme cases, the pre-war periods. Many reconstruction projects, therefore, erase what remains of the built environment in the name of 'worlding' and 'globalizing' the city. Political and economic elites and architects see in real estate and property a chance to attract investors and tourists. As a result, they propose new ways of living and new architectural styles that enable the construction of luxurious high-rise buildings, tower blocks, malls and entertainment facilities targeted at foreigners and the local rich, not the impacted and suffering people. Cities become sites for profit, not for people. In these efforts, an entire way of living is destroyed as the familiar street patterns, local shops, architecture style, and beloved spaces and places are razed to the ground in the name of reconstruction. Reconstruction can be the new form of domicide that might destroy more than the war itself.

Politicians, architects and urban planners see in the reconstruction an opportunity to impose their visions. Even when driven by 'good intentions', reconstruction might lead to the loss of a city's cultural heritage sites and to the radical transformation in the way people orient themselves, experience and navigate their built environments. Many cities have witnessed similar approaches throughout history. In Coventry, there was an enthusiasm for a 'modernist' approach to planning, which was translated into a rejection of what is old in the city. In 1945, the *Coventry of the Future* exhibition brought with it proposals with rigid lines, spaciousness, speed, cleanliness and order. When reconstruction started in the city, many of its still-standing buildings were demolished. The irregular streetscape was replaced with a newly ordered grid, laying the foundation for a new centre, the Precinct. It was a moment that transformed the image of the city. Recent scholarly work unveiled the reaction of people towards the new visions, and how it was opposed by many residents who submitted letters against the reconstruction of the city centre. But despite these letters, the project went ahead. The decades following the end of the war witnessed the demolition of much of the city's mediaeval character, with disorientating experiences for Coventrians who lament the loss to their city (Webb 2018).

Little has been written about this destructive aspect of Coventry's reconstruction and its impact on the people of the city. Hubbard, Faire and Lilley (2003: 391), however, interviewed people who experienced this transformation of Coventry. In their research, they bring the voices of those who lament the old city centre. As one of the residents recalled his experience in the newly built city centre:

> As I was growing up I disliked the precinct. I couldn't accept it . . . I didn't like this vast distance from one wall to the other. And it wasn't because I had to walk so far across to get from one shop to the other, it just didn't have any character. I thought it was so bland, it was so plain and ordinary and there was nothing – I mean they kept putting little flower plots and raised beds and you had say, well, why? Well it was only to break up the concrete. It was a concrete city centre. (Hubbard, Faire and Lilley 2003: 391)

In Gernika and Coventry, we see how the built environment is lost once in the time of war and then again in the name of reconstruction. For people who witnessed the trauma of war, further losses and damage to their towns and cities are experienced in the aftermath of the war. In cities that witnessed radical destruction to their social, cultural and built environments in Iraq and Syria in the past decade, there are fears that new domicidal projects will be implemented in the name of reconstruction. In Mosul, Iraq, there are concerns that future reconstruction plans will destroy the city's historical identity and erase the memory of the city instead of preserving it. In Beirut, after the tragic port explosion in 2020, there are fears of a duplication of the approach adopted following the Civil War, a 'Solidere 2.0' (Bulos 2020), in reference to Solidere. Architecture, engineering and construction companies that might not have any attachment to these places nor have an understanding of the suffering of the impacted communities, might with 'good intentions' cause more suffering and damage. In the quest of building a new world, geographies of inequalities are cemented as reconstruction projects focus on selective sites. Reconstruction, therefore, can become a political and economic tool that destroys what remains of past ways of living in the aftermath of conflicts.

When reconstruction is selective regarding who to reconstruct for and where, new dividing lines emerge, not only physically in towns and cities, but also socially between communities; those who benefit from the reconstruction, and those who are left behind. Unjust reconstruction threatens the resilience of cities (Vale 2014). For instance, after the conflict in Timor-Leste (East Timor) in 1999, attention was directed towards the capital Dili in attempts to link the city to the global economy. This neoliberal approach to the reconstruction of the capital neglected the needs of the local people and paid little attention to poverty alleviation. Through focusing reconstruction on specific geographies, Dili began to emerge as a disembodied city, distinct from the national territory (Beall, Goodfellow and Rodgers 2013).

Today, similar fears and anxieties emerge with the current reconstruction debates in Syria. As seen in different cities around the world at different points in time, reconstruction is not necessarily a means to an end to the urban trauma and misery, nor is it a means to an end to conflict. Reconstruction can bring new seeds of urban struggle and crises to communities whose lives have been shattered by trauma, loss, urban violence and displacement. There are fears that the reconstruction of Syria will be the new landscape of contestation, the new site of struggle, and that reconstruction will be used as punishment to residents who oppose those in political power (HRW 2014, 2019; Imady 2019). There are fears that new destructive reconstruction plans will erase what remains of Syria's built environment, removing its layers of memory and identity.

Emerging debates on Syria's future reconstruction

At the time of domicide in Syria, academics, architects and activists working on the built environment have been talking about domicide, displacement, reconstruction and rebuilding (Rabbat 2016; Harastani and Hanna 2019; Al Asali 2020). This has led to the emergence of several initiatives, projects, research papers and films that explore the relationship between domicide and cities. In their work, diasporic architects have attempted to respond to some of the most pressing questions that face our villages, towns and cities: what is to be done to provide shelter for the rising number of people who lost their homes? And how can the lost memory be protected so that it can influence future reconstruction? These questions, and many others, have been researched and explored by individuals as well as groups around the world (Said and Yazigi 2018; DiNapoli 2019; Imady 2019; Al-Sabouni 2021). I have personally been contacted or have had the chance to meet with architects and engineers who grew up in Syria and now reside in different cities across the world, such as Beirut, Cairo, Dubai, Istanbul, Jeddah, Berlin, Cambridge and Budapest. All of them feel the responsibility to think about their own city or village (read the reflections on reconstruction by three UK-based Syrians in Box 4.1). All of them feel the urge to respond to the destruction of architecture. Even those who never lived in Syria but are the children of Syrian families who live abroad have been keen to contribute to the debate on architecture and domicide. Once, I was contacted by a woman based in Saudi Arabia who wanted to work on the heritage of Aleppo's houses but explained that she never lived in Syria and had no strong knowledge of the country.

> **BOX 4.1** Reflections on the future reconstruction.
>
> When thinking about the reconstruction of Syria, the first thing I envision is a scenario where all Syrians work and collaborate to create cities for everyone to dwell and prosper. I do not think returning to the pre-conflict setting should be considered an option, I believe that rebuilding Syria should be carried out with a vision that reflects on the mistakes of our pre-conflict cities and aim for a more healthy and sustainable future. I share the hope of many Syrians that rebuilding Syria would encompass creating inclusive cities, restoring our rich and versatile heritage and celebrating the uniqueness and identity of our cities. Parallel to that, I see that reconstruction needs to be rooted in a plan to protect our country against the potential threats of

climate change. This scenario might sound complex to achieve, however, it is not difficult if we adopt a collaborative approach to lead the recovery process.

Many elements define a successful post-conflict recovery. However, one key principle I consider vital to rebuilding Syria is 'Participation'. Adopting a top-down approach is unlikely to be the most effective approach to reconstruction. Syria needs a bidirectional approach where a sustainable comprehensive plan is integrated with the engagement of all Syrians and stakeholders. Rebuilding efforts should carry the vision of all Syrians and allow all Syrians to participate. When people collaborate in rebuilding their cities, they would create architecture they believe is worth preserving and worth maintaining. Participation would increase people's sense of belonging and ownership to their cities. This sense of ownership would make cities more resilient to future conflicts. When society is a partner in reconstruction, this would lead to creating healthier cities and erecting architecture worth fighting for in the future.

The environmental framework under which reconstruction functions needs to be strategic and comprehensive. In order to create a sustainable future, we need to implement environmental policies that could manage the noticeable environmental impact of conflict as well as increase the climate change resilience of our cities and urban areas. I believe that reconstruction should be endorsed with a national climate change mitigation planning to avoid repercussions that would be difficult to manage.

Syria's recovery needs to utilize the efforts of its people and take advantage of the technological advancement in the field of construction and other sectors. Reconstruction, as challenging as it might seem, presents an opportunity to rebuild a better future for everyone and avoid future conflicts.

Karam Alkatlabe, PhD candidate, University of Cambridge

What happened in Syria was not a natural disaster that we now have to rebuild. I feel it is about the revolution, conflict, war, and there is a crack in the country between people and there is destruction. So, for me reconstruction, the last thing is about the stones. Reconstruction is about reconstructing the Syrian society where people are divided, and families are split and between the different generations in the country and between those who agreed to bomb areas and those living in these areas. There is a need to reconstruct the entire society.

To architects, don't treat people as plastic Lego figures that you put them in your project . . . People are not Lego figures to put in a Lego house. People have dreams, fears, miseries, and aspirations. If you want people to come and live in their areas, then they have an imagination of their own areas and homes. If you really want to bring people to their areas of origin, then you need to ask them about the relationship between these people and the building they will live in. For whom is this reconstruction? For the rich who can afford to live in these areas? Why don't we have surveys; institutions in each neighbourhood, a voting system which asks people what they would prefer and discusses the proposal with them; someone to explain this project to them and respect their opinion.

Sana Kikhia, Syrian activist

Look at Dubai, there are skyscrapers, but little is known about the local community and the small markets and shops of the city. I don't want to feel as a stranger in my city. I want people to be involved in shaping the future reconstruction of Syria; ask people how was their home, can we build something similar? I can't imagine living in another house than mine in Syria. But what people would say if they have lost their home? The connection to home is not only physical or emotional, we're unconsciously attached to our 'home'.

We want the ordinary people of the city and the architects and planners. If you want the ordinary people to be engaged and get an authentic solution after digging, you can find people through social media to reach out to more people and engage with them or even better live from the ground. Maybe one could create a platform online to start creating a dialogue. Focus groups could be great, but to engage with more people who were displaced internally and externally, online engagement could be the start of a solution. But even some people in camps might have no internet, other people in camps might struggle to speak about their own experiences.

I want people to participate in shaping the future of their cities. I want people to come to their ruined areas and talk about their neighbourhood; about their memory and the places that mattered to them. For me, I want the bakery shop, the doctor, the things that we are used to go to. Make people participate. I love public spaces, gardens, areas for children, cafes, these tiny little spaces. You want people to come back together and after all what we have been through, there is so much distance between people, and each is conferenced about their own selves, but you want people to come and share experiences, none has not suffered in this war.

Hiba Abo Slo, London-based assistant planner from Syria

In the UK, where I have lived since 2011, there have been several workshops, webinars, conferences and initiatives organized and led mainly or partially by UK-based Syrian activists, architects and engineers. Many of these events and gatherings have been widely attended by individuals who studied for their first degree in Syria before moving to the UK to carry on with their Masters and/or PhDs. These meetings were put together to connect architects, engineers and activists, exchange knowledge, learn from one another and explore different areas of work on responses to destruction and displacement in Syria. Some of these meetings also included presentations by Syrians who do not work on Syria projects but wish to share their knowledge and skills with their fellow architects. I attended several events that explored different themes such as refugee camps, reconstruction and housing. Since there is no physical community centre for the Syrian community in London and with the Syrian Embassy in the UK being closed for several years now, these meetings took place in different venues.

The types of interventions in Syria's reconstruction varied not only in scope, method and approach, but also in scale, medium and focus. Houda Jwadi, a London-based Syrian urban researcher who completed her Master's degree at University College London, worked on videos titled *The City Talks*, which include interviews with London-based Syrian architects on their response to domicide. Shahd Mousalli and Tameem Emam, who both reside in the UK, founded HLP Maps and registered it as a social enterprise in the UK in 2020. As millions of people are displaced from their homes in Syria, and with the destruction of homes, there are fears of the loss of property rights. Mousalli and Emam attempt to engage with refugees and IDPs to document their property rights that are under threat. Together, Mousalli and Emam have undertaken several workshops with communities, including those who reside in the UK. One of these workshops, for instance, was part of the Celebrating Syria Festival in 2019.

In 2015, the Arab Reform Initiative (ARI), an independent Arab think tank based in France, set up the Tahdir for Syria programme (Tahdir in Arabic means 'preparation'). According to ARI, Tahdir is designed to build capacity in three fields widely considered as fundamental to post-conflict reconstruction (Arab Reform Initiative 2015). The programme was implemented in early 2016. Bassma Kodmani, a co-founder of the ARI and its former Executive Director, released a message on the training programme, explaining how it is aimed at bringing the knowledge to people's homes wherever they are – inside or outside Syria – instead of asking people to travel to undertake training (Tahdir4Syria 2017). The training programme has three rounds, using both online learning material and face-to-face meetings. The programme attracted Syrians based in different countries. In the third round, 106 participants were accepted; 71 of whom resided inside Syria, 31 in Türkiye and the rest in Lebanon, Holland and France. The programme delivers three main courses: Security Sector Reform and Justice; Local Administration and Decentralization; and Architecture, Urban Development – Sustainable Reconstruction. Several Syrian architects living abroad have taken part in developing some of the curriculum material of the programme.

Before the start of the Syrian Revolution, there was no programme at any university inside Syria dealing with questions of violence and cities, destruction and reconstruction. This has been the case, even though Syria has historically witnessed cycles of violence and destruction as in the domicide of Hama in the early 1980s. Furthermore, geographically, Syria is located between several countries that witnessed domicide, such as in Lebanon's Civil War and the invasion of Iraq by the US in 2003. Today, however, an increasing number of Syrian architects (and more broadly, those working in the built environment sector) are revisiting past conflicts to explore how cities have been destroyed and reconstructed.

The publications, initiatives and projects that emerged outside Syria have been different from those that emerged inside Syria. Many of those who left the country have focused on the relationship between politics, violence and the built environment. By doing so, they highlighted the weaponization of architecture and urban planning and explored topics that those who are inside Syria might be unable to raise. An example of such writing is an excellent series of articles titled 'Weaponised Urbanism' (Abou Zainedin 2019), published in Arabic by *Al-Jumhuriya*, a platform that was founded by a group of Syrian writers and academics in 2012. The series, which was edited by Sawsan Abou Zainedin, a Syrian architect and urban development planner based in London, includes six articles written by six different authors who reside in the UK, Sweden and France. Six themes were introduced in this series which show the weaponization of architecture, urban planning and cultural heritage. Themes in the series included: the relationship between urbanism, power and fear; the production of homogenous urbanism as a form of cleansing; the use of checkpoints as part of conflict infrastructure (such as walls, fences and barriers); the emerging laws and decrees to legitimize urban violence; and the role of international organizations as partners with the regime in Syria. The articles were accompanied by the work of two artists who produced black and white drawings (Figure 4.1). One of these drawings, Figure 4.2, symbolically reflects the destruction of the built environment. It shows a tank moving forwards as buildings on either side of it are being destroyed. Two buildings are shown crumbling into ruins, each of them is turned literally upside down, whilst the buildings that are still standing are being shown to have a similar fate.

Dilemmas of reconstruction

Inside Syria, the emergence of the debates on reconstruction brings up challenging dilemmas. There are fears that reconstruction will be concomitant with new waves of forced displacement, re-destruction and urban violence. Reconstruction, often seen as a source of hope to 'raise cities from the ashes', has started to appear as a tool for punishment, destruction and displacement (Azzouz 2020b). Whilst conflict frontlines have been shifting

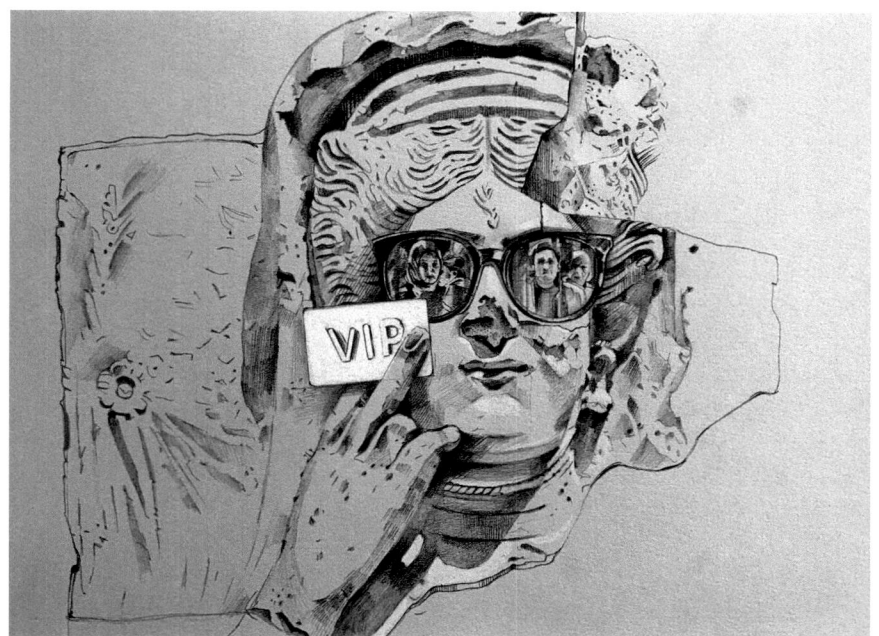

FIGURE 4.1 *Weaponized Urbanism*, 2019.
Source: Aliaa Aboukhaddour, Yasmeen Fanari for aljumhuriya.net (2019).

FIGURE 4.2 *Weaponized Urbanism*, 2019.
Source: Aliaa Aboukhaddour, Yasmeen Fanari for aljumhuriya.net (2019).

across Syria with different political actors controlling different parts of the country, discussions and proposals have emerged inside and outside Syria on the future reconstruction. Many of these emerging debates and visions have either focused on monumental cultural heritage sites such as the questions surrounding the reconstruction of Palmyra (Harrowell 2016; Munawar 2017; Thompson 2017), or on proposals that call for replacing 'informal' and 'illegal' neighbourhoods with luxurious copies of tower blocks. Reconstructing the ordinary, the lesser known, the domestic, the everyday urban life, the sense of community and neighbourhood has been rarely discussed.

Current emerging debates on reconstruction are significantly shaped by the political and economic elites and the new emerging warlords. These debates are also shaped and influenced by local and/or international architects, planners, writers and academics. Some of these projects are already commissioned by the Syrian government, such as their agreements with Russia's archaeological projects in Palmyra (Hardan 2021) and projects that have been commissioned in Damascus, e.g. the Marota City. Other debates, however, have not been commissioned but are led by international organizations, think tanks and academic institutions that have the funding and interest in reconstruction.

These projects bring with them several dilemmas. One of them is the lack of engagement with Syrians who are supposed to be the beneficiaries of these projects. In most of these debates, the voice of ordinary people is lost, neglecting their suffering and needs. I once attended a lecture by a Syrian architect who argued that the work of an architect is like the work of a surgeon. According to her, ordinary people know nothing about surgery and hence should not be involved. People who lost everything, who have suffered so much, who live their everyday life struggling to access their basic needs, feel so powerless and unheard, not only by politicians and the rich elites, but also by some of the local architects who work as if they live in a separate universe.

Many architects see in wartime destruction an 'opportunity' to erase what remains in the city and start again with a clean-slate approach. As a result, they propose radical approaches towards reconstruction that erases the old buildings and roads and replace them with more spacious streets and tower blocks. For these individuals, the destruction that took place during the years of war should be followed by mass destruction of the remnants of older parts of the city. This is something I heard from an architect in Homs who had lived in the Old City, in-between these small alleyways but now wished to erase these memories. Some Syrian architects who currently reside in Dubai, Doha and Riyadh, see no harm in destroying Homs' heart and in building shopping centres such as the ones they see in the cities where they now reside. There is no doubt that many people from Homs see in the destruction a solution to critical urban issues, and that erasing what remains can 'fix' these issues (e.g. the lack of public spaces, green areas and a sustainable transportation system).

One of the proposals for the future reconstruction of Homs suggested building a new Homs outside the city. Ghassan Jansiz, an architect based in Homs, published his proposal at the Royal Institute of British Architects (RIBA) titled: '*Start Again: Let's Ditch Homs and Build a New One*' (2014). In his proposal, he makes an analogy between the city and a 'dead body'. He shows a map of a 'new Homs' that is located outside of Homs, on its western side by the petrol refinery. This proposal, which is 'different from what everybody else is considering', is actually very similar to what was planned before the war. An unpublished report by the Syrian German Technical Cooperation in 2009 proposed an expansion to Homs in the same area referred to by Jansiz. Furthermore, Jansiz also proposed the transformation of the old parts of Homs into traditional markets and hotels. It is a reconstruction that calls for leaving the city and building a new one. In his own words, Jansiz notes:

> I realise the radical nature of my suggestion and what a shock it would be for many. However, with a little bit of calmness and thinking, its logic becomes clear. Think of it as you would any case of clinical death when there's absolutely no use in keeping the life-support machines on, and money and effort are wasted. Facing the bitterness of reality is the perfect way to treat it. Trying to pump life into a dead body instead of picking up the life just next to it is totally in vain. So, I ask, isn't it more rational, more appropriate to declare the death of Old Homs and look for the birth of New Homs?

There are local and international voices calling for the recreation of Beirut's city centre reconstruction or for the Dubaization of cities, the use of Dubai as a model to shape cities. Fears of the Dubai model do not come from nowhere, and nor are they new (Abaza 2011). They are in fact rather old and rooted in pre-war plans and visions that were proposed to transform the urban, social and cultural fabrics of different cities in Syria. These pre-war plans and projects (e.g. the Homs Dream project that I explored in Chapter 2) seem to be re-emerging now and might become more powerful in future reconstruction. The Homs City Council announced that the 'Homs Dream' project has not been cancelled, but rather, it will be edited and worked on for the future reconstruction (Business 2 Business 2019). Such a project will benefit the rich and elites and neglect the poor and the marginalized. There are different reasons why these projects will once again emerge. First, cultural capital will be needed, and real estate projects will be seen as a platform to recover a collapsed economy. Second, there will be a lack of technical and architectural skills due to the displacement of over half of the population, and these projects have already been planned and designed and are 'ready' to be implemented. Third, the Syrian government will see a chance to implement such projects after they were opposed by many Syrians before the war. As people are displaced, this will be the chance for the government to impose these plans in the name of reconstruction.

Pre-2011 urban plans will reshape the historical cities in Syria following the model of other cities in the Gulf Region, such as Dubai. In her article, 'Dubai on Barada? The Making of "Globalised Damascus" in Times of Urban Crisis', Leïla Vignal (2016) looks at some of the pre-war architecture projects in Damascus between 2000 and 2010 (one of these projects advanced to construction in 2010). In her article, Vignal explores how the Dubai model was reflected in Damascus before the war with the local government's desire to respond to some of the urban crises on the one hand, and to attract big investments, mainly from the Gulf property developers, on the other hand. Tower blocks, expensive hotels and restaurants, gated communities with lavish apartments, swimming pools and outdoor sports facilities were proposed. One of these projects, Yaafur, was located outside Damascus, which is densely populated and crowded, and led to the creation of a new, socially exclusive city for the privileged, far from the decaying, crowded Damascus. It seems that the years of war have been the years to bring these projects back into the conversation.

Reconstruction for the chosen few

Even in the time of war, when millions of Syrians are displaced from their homes, and people are struggling with their everyday lives and the country is drowning in poverty, projects that were on hold for the past decade have re-emerged. One of these projects is Park Residence Yaafour, by Kuwait Syrian Holding. Yaafour is located around 26 km from the heart of Damascus. A video that was released in December 2018 shows not only a glimpse of the project design which includes 71 residential buildings (1,174 apartments), but also a walk through the buildings and the activities that will take place in the gated community, an entire way of living for the rich and elite is illustrated (Park Residence Yaafour 2018). The video shows a life that does not relate to the reality of the lives of millions of people living in extreme poverty: expensive cars are driven through the gate of the project, men and women wearing tiny shorts are running and cycling, kids are drawing in graffiti zones, yogees are by the water reflecting on their life and its tranquillity, families are gathering to eat outdoors, whilst a table with champagne is featured, fountains are everywhere, swimming pools are at the heart of the project, with a woman in a swimsuit, a topless muscled man doing chin-ups in an outdoor gym and two other men playing basketball.

So happy, so joyful, so peaceful, so proud, so rich, so healthy, so powerful, so unreal. They are unlike those living in refugee camps in extreme poverty or those internally displaced Syrians cramped in ruined buildings, struggling to find shelter. They seem to be in a utopian world, out of place, out of war, out of the misery that has broken the lives and dreams of millions of us. But this imagined life seems real to the current lives of the super-rich and warlords in Syria. It is a surreal video that creates a landscape of forgetting.

The project seems to be in a utopian place, not in a conflicted country where more than 14 million people are displaced and many are struggling to get bread due to the collapse of the country's economy. It is a disconnection from reality and a destructive project that will benefit the very few, separating them within a gate from the everyday harsh reality of Damascus. As their gated community closes its gates, it is separated from the people who do not deserve to be there, those who should live ruined lives in ruined apartments. Globally, gated and enclosed communities are by no means new. Gates are not only promoted to enhance security, but also reflect the urge to self-segregate, the eagerness for prestige (Cséfalvay 2011). Gates do not only maintain but they also increase segregation. Researchers have highlighted the challenges and problems of the securitization of space. Among these concerns are the creation of a socially and spatially fragmented urban landscape as people separate themselves from 'others' (Tedong, Grant and Wan Abd Aziz 2015). For those who choose to live within these gated communities, the primary motivations are not only safety but also the display of status and the real and symbolic separation from the non-residents of these spaces (Wu and Pow 2010). This is the separation that is featured in the video in Damascus where residents are gated from the damaged world outside their gates.

People featured in the film also look like the people who deserve to live in these places. None of the women featured in the film has a headscarf, unlike many of the women who live in misery and poverty in refugee camps in Lebanon and Jordan. These are the 'modern' and 'developed' homogenous Syrians who deserve to live in this 'modern' and 'developed' gated project. It is a design for the chosen few, for a selected slice of the country (and probably wealthy people and allies from overseas) who distance themselves from the harsh reality. On their Facebook page, the Park Residence Yaafour uses the hashtag #ItsTimeForHome. Of course, it is time for home, but a home for whom? 'When you own a home in Park Residence Yaafour,' they add on Facebook, 'you belong to a vibrant community with a dynamic lifestyle that few places can match.' Images on their Instagram account in December 2020 show that some buildings are already under construction. This gives us an example of some of the emerging luxury projects that are promoted as 'progressive' solutions to the urban crises, whilst neglecting those unprivileged and poor, and those marginalized from the political and economic power.

Marota City is another project in Damascus that sparked outrage among residents, architects, human rights organizations, urban scholars and activists. It even got international coverage in the news media because of the fears and violence this project brought with it (Khattab and Cornish 2018; Harastani and Hanna 2019; HRW 2019; Loveluck 2019). Led by Damascus Cham Holding Company, the project, similar to Park Residence Yaafour, presents a lifestyle for the wealthy, with six shopping centres and a mall, a theatre, twisted high-rise buildings, twin towers, hospitals and business centres. The project is full of giant towers that oversee Mount Qasioun, three of them – proposed as landmarks – have 70 floors, as high as the mountain. People interested in living in Marota City are shown a 3D modelled environment and potential activities in their newly built neighbourhood: a woman in a bikini is swimming in the rooftop pool of her residential building whilst her neighbours are sitting relaxed and are enjoying the view of Damascus. Another woman is looking at some architectural drawings on her computer, whilst another is running. None of these women are wearing a headscarf as in Yaafour, cementing an image of how one should look when living there.

Unlike the Yaafour project that is located just outside Damascus, Marota City has a significant location inside Damascus, very close to Umayyad Square, the Ministry of Higher Education, the Ministry of Defence, the National Library, the Opera House, the university and other important areas of the city. The naming of the project itself also requires reflection. It includes the word *City*, as if those who live there will have their own *city* within the City of Damascus, segregating themselves from those who are outside this elitist *city*. The entire project is designed with a green belt around it. The word Marota is also symbolic as it means sovereignty in the Syriac Aramaic language. In an interview on Syrian TV, the CEO of the project explained how they changed the name of the original area, Basateen El-Razi, a neighbourhood that was completely wiped out to lay the foundations for the Marota City. He highlighted that the word City was added to the project name, although it is just a neighbourhood, not a city. Marota City is built on the destruction of people's homes, but even the name of this neighbourhood has been wiped out along with its architecture.

Through complete destruction, the new urban world of Marota City is built on the wreckage of the old one; it is built on the homes of people who lived in the neighbourhood. Basateen El-Razi residents were not displaced because of the fighting or shelling, but in the name of redevelopment that literally wiped out their neighbourhood. Satellite images show the entire erasure of the neighbourhood, including people's homes and agrarian land (Figure 4.3). The

DOMICIDAL RECONSTRUCTION

(a)

(b)

FIGURE 4.3 (*a*) Basateen El-Razi, 2012 and (*b*) 2019.
Source: Google Earth.

empty land looks like a striking void in Damascus. The project has made little progress as it has been impacted by the political situation and economic collapse in the country. Marota City raises questions about the timing of the destruction in a country where millions of people are already displaced from their home. It also raises questions about class, power and the emergence of new warlords who benefit from these projects at the expense of the suffering of the poor.

In a city where the gap between the rich and poor is widening, projects such as Marota City come to solidify and even further widen this gap. Those who suffer the most from this project are the people who lived in this area. Their way of life has been destroyed and their right to their property is threatened by new laws and decrees that were formulated in the past decade. Those who have documentation to prove they own a property there are given shares in the city, but many of the people who lived in the neighbourhood for decades have no such documentation as the neighbourhood included 'informal' housing of those who migrated in the past from the countryside to the orchards. Furthermore, many of those who have sufficient documentation will not be able to afford having their own home in the newly built area. The CEO explains in the same TV interview that people who lived there will automatically have their own home, but they need to pay for its 'construction and completion'. What they need to pay to live in the homes they were kicked out from is beyond the realm of reality for many people who are drowning in poverty.

Such projects are possible through the new laws and decrees established during the war. This includes Decree No. 66 authorized by the government to redevelop 'informal' areas in the city, such as Basateen El-Razi. Law No. 10 was later announced to expand the geography of Decree No. 66 to include the entire country, rather than Damascus only. Other former rebel-held areas are threatened with demolition and new domicidal projects, for example in Barzeh, Jobar, Daraya and Qaboun. Fear grows amongst residents and displaced Syrians with the emergence of these laws and decrees. Under Law 10, people initially had 30 days to prove their ownership, but this was an impossible mission due to different reasons such as forced displacement and loss of documentation. It was then increased to a year. If a person fails to show the required documentation, ownership will be transferred to the local government. Critics have seen in the project a tool to change the demography by using land and property as a weapon (Arab News 2018). This is why organizations, including The Day After (TDA), which I mentioned in the Introduction, are working on recording HLP documents of displaced people. In March 2022, TDA organized its first HLP conference in Istanbul, unpacking different themes related to transitional justice, refugees' right to return and the protection of property rights for women. Other organizations, such as the

Norwegian Refugee Council, publish their work on HLP and the challenges faced by Syrian refugees, including civil registration for families with missing relatives, issues of death registration and access to legal identity and civil documentation. The question of HLP will remain central to the process of transitional justice and reconstruction, and should be kept at the heart of any future reconstruction projects so that the HLP rights of people are preserved and protected.

Reconstruction as a weapon

During the past decade, urban planning and architecture have been used, abused and misused in Syria. They have been weaponized to destroy people's homes, not only for 'military purposes' or against the 'war on terror', which have been the 'justifications' in many cases, but also, in the name of urban planning that targeted 'informal' areas of the urban poor. This has been explicitly researched by several scholars, activists, lawyers and architects who focused particularly on the relationship between informal housing and domicide. Among these scholars is Valérie Clerc, a Research Fellow at the French National Research Institute for Sustainable Development (IRD), based in Paris. In her work, Clerc (2014: 45) focuses on the policies towards informal settlement before and after the conflict, making a link between pre- and post-2011 urban planning policies towards informal housing. Clerc explains how the targeting of 'informal' settlements through urban policies started in the 2000s. Back then, the reform of the legislative urban framework, with the assistance of international organizations, encouraged the upgrading and renewal of informal areas. During the time of the conflict, these urban options were brought back to the table. Several areas were bulldozed when the marginalized people were already struggling with extreme poverty and hardship. Clerc explained how these demolitions were selective to certain areas in which 'government forces and affiliated militia intentionally burned and destroyed the homes and businesses believed to belong to suspected anti-government activists and their supporters during the raids'.

Whilst much attention has been focused on the impact of new laws and decrees on informal housing, as in Marota City and other luxury reconstruction projects in Damascus (Harastani and Hanna 2019), little attention has been directed towards the destruction of housing in other parts of Syria. Hama is one of these cities that suffered the complete destruction of entire neighbourhoods. Between September and October 2012, the Syrian authorities deliberately demolished the Masha' al-Arb'een neighbourhood in the north of Hama, and between April and May 2013, the Wadi al-Jouz neighbourhood located in the north-west of Hama. The Syrian government claimed that these were efforts to implement urban planning laws and remove illegally constructed buildings. Pro-government news channels claimed that these demolitions of thousands of homes were made to restore peace and security and remove urban irregularities. Human Rights Watch (2014) issued a report that specifically focuses on these two neighbourhoods in Hama (and also in Damascus). In their report, *Razed to the Ground*, HRW documented large-scale demolitions that violate laws of war as they serve no necessary military purpose. They also interviewed residents who had their homes destroyed. One of them said:

> We saw bulldozers approaching our neighborhood, but we stayed in our house because we never thought that they would destroy all the houses. After two days, our turn came. We left our things. We were afraid to stay one second longer because our house was shaking while bulldozers destroyed the houses close by. When the bulldozers approached our house, my husband went outside to talk with the army soldiers. My husband was begging them to spare our house but they shouted: 'We want to destroy, we want to destroy.' They didn't explain to us what was happening. (HRW 2014: 13)

As if the demolitions of these thousands of homes were not enough, domicide continued in Hama at the time when the conflict frontlines were still moving across the country. In September 2018, the Hama Governorate decided to demolish the Al-Naqarneh neighbourhood south of the city. A video on the Hama Governorate social media page released in November 2019 showed the governer, Muhammad Krishati, visiting the neighbourhod. He is featured in the video, supervising the demolition of a home by a bulldozer in Hama, as reported by Enab Baladi, a Syrian non-profit media organization (Enab Baladi 2020). The emerging laws and decrees that allow the demolition of 'unlicensed' and 'illegal' homes seem both selective and symbolic. They are selective as many pro-government housing areas, like Haret Al-Tabb and Al-Tiyyar in Hama, are equally categorized as 'informal', and yet they have been kept intact (*The Syria Report* 2021b). These demolitions are the sites of punishment, where those who are not needed in the country are not only displaced, but also have their homes razed to the ground.

The weaponization of land and property rights has taken different ways and forms to target, destroy, cleanse and gain revenue. Jon D. Unruh (2016: 453) has identified seven ways in which the Syrian government is using land and property right systems in its 'military-on-civilian engagements': (1) destroy and target HLP records and administrative infrastructure; (2) identify and target anti-government places; (3) target and destroy the HLP belongings of the opponents; (4) confiscate, relocate and transact at HLP and issue forced documentation;

(5) confiscate HLP documents at checkpoints; (6) derive significant revenue for the war effort; and (7) use state laws to effect displays and gain position of HLP. Urban planning and policies for the future reconstruction might follow similar patterns of weaponization. The future reconstruction might wipe out entire areas, and this would be seen as a continuation of not only what has been erased during the years of conflict, but also as an expansion to the plans and policies that first emerged in early 2000s; plans and policies that further marginalize the marginalized and push them out of their homes and cities. Domicide will be reconstructed, this time not by bombing and tanks, but by bulldozers in the name of reconstruction and the erasure of 'unlicensed' buildings.

It is important that writings have emerged on the weaponization of reconstruction, but sometimes it is repetitive as writers recycle published statements and repeat the same arguments and revisit the same dilemmas. What has been missing, and what is greatly needed today, is to think of points of action; awareness should be one of these points. Future publications of academics and policy-makers should raise awareness about the destructiveness approach of reconstruction before bulldozers and major companies come to erase what remains of our cities and villages. Scholars, journalists, activists, writers and researchers are pushing on different fronts to warn about violent reconstruction. For instance, in May 2019 at the Massachusetts Institute of Technology (MIT), Nasser Rabbat and Deen Sharp organized a two-day symposium, *Reconstruction as Violence*, that focused on how violence not only destroys but also constitutes, designs and organizes the built environment. Many Syrian architects across the world are writing in both Arabic and English to raise awareness about the violence of reconstruction and its impact on communities.

In addition to legal questions surrounding HLP rights, there are several concerns regarding the reconstruction economy. Who will fund the reconstruction? How will the funds be spent? Would they be directed towards rebuilding houses and infrastructure projects for the millions of people who lost their homes? Or will these funds be manipulated and spent selectively? Today, out of Syria's chaos and destruction, businessmen are building fortunes through the profits they are making from the reconstruction efforts in Syria (Rasmussen and Osseiran 2018). Reconstruction funds will be collected, but for whom? In 2014, the Syrian Reconstruction Committee was established following the introduction of a reconstruction tax in July 2013. At the start, the tax was 5 per cent but it was then increased to 10 per cent in 2017. At a time when millions of people are living in poverty and their homes are destroyed, they have to pay for these taxes in the name of 'reconstruction' that promises their homes will be rebuilt. However, a report that was released in 2021 showed little evidence that the money has been spent helping civilians (Bassiki and Mathiason 2021).

The Syrian government has repeatedly announced that priority for future reconstruction will be given to those who supported Syria, and 'definitely China, Russia and Iran' (SANA 2019). Iran, which supported the Syrian government during the war years, has expressed interest in Syria's reconstruction. This interest has unfolded in different ways. In April 2021, the first reconstruction conference was organized as a collaboration between Iran and Syria at Aleppo University (Shahoud 2021). The chancellor of the university, Maher Karman, explained the importance of learning from Iran when reconstructing the Old City of Aleppo. In May 2021, an Iranian consulate was opened in Aleppo. Faisal Mekdad, the Syrian foreign minister and former Permanent Envoy to the United Nations, delivered a speech online, explaining that the opening 'reflects deep relations between the two countries and highlights the economic development which Aleppo has witnessed since its liberation until today in terms of reconstruction and repairing what has been destroyed by terrorism'. Iran, which has established a strong presence in the countries neighbouring Syria, i.e Iraq and Lebanon, is also keen to connect this presence through Syria. Iranian Foreign Minister Mohammad Javad Zarif also delivered an online speech at the event, noting that the opening of the consulate in Aleppo 'indicates the attention we pay to this city in terms of history and culture, and cooperation between the two countries' (Qriema 2021).

Other countries that have been supporting the Syrian regime have also been part of the conversation on reconstruction. For instance, in 2016, China's Special Envoy for Syria Xie Xiaoyan said that China is ready to work with countries such as Russia in the post-war reconstruction of Syria (Sabbagh 2016). In 2019, Chinese Deputy Minister of Foreign Affairs Chen Xiaodong met in Beijing with Syrian Presidential, Political and Media Adviser Dr Bouthaina Shaaban. During the meeting, Xiaoyan expressed the readiness of China to offer economic support to Syria and the willingness to participate in its reconstruction process (Al-Jazaeri 2019). Despite all the killing, destruction and displacement they caused in the past decade, Russia urges the international community to support the reconstruction process in Syria and blames the US for preventing the reconstruction through its sanctions. Sanctions have been imposed on individuals benefitting the regime. For instance, in 2017, the US imposed sanctions on sixteen individuals, including those investing in luxury reconstruction projects on land seized by the Syrian regime from the people (Reuters 2019). Russia does not seem to provide money for reconstruction but is keen to make money out of the reconstruction. Despite their political involvement in Syria, Russia is now attempting to make the case that reconstruction is not political and that governments should award funds for the reconstruction. The Russian ambassador to Canada, Oleg Stepanov, said in November 2021 that 'it is incorrect to link the provision of reconstruction assistance to the Syrians to certain political conditions and requirements', directing his conversation mainly to the 'West' which rejects participating in Syria's reconstruction without it undergoing a political change (Othman and Al-Jazaeri 2021).

Reconstructing cultural heritage

Emerging debates on the future reconstruction of Syria have not been limited to mega-luxury residential projects, but also include cultural heritage sites. In Homs, several projects have emerged focusing on some of the symbolic sites and buildings, including mosques, churches, souks and public squares. The focus on selective symbolic sites has been used as a platform to demonstrate that life has returned to Homs. However, when speaking to the local Homsis who remain in the city, one of their main concerns is to have their own shelter before the rehabilitation of any monument or symbolic building. An example of these projects is the rehabilitation of the Khalid ibn al-Walid Mosque, an iconic mosque in Homs in the Al Khalidiya neighbourhood. It was shelled in 2013. Figure 4.4 shows the damage caused to the mosque after the neighbourhood was captured by the Syrian Army and the siege of the Old City ended. The mosque has now been rehabilitated almost as if nothing had happened. In 2019, Chechnya's chief mufti, Salah Mezhiyev, attended the opening ceremony of the mosque and cut the ribbon at the entrance with the

(a)   (b)

FIGURE 4.4 Damage to the Khalid ibn al-Walid Mosque, 2014 (*a*) and (*b*).
Source: Omama Zankawan, taken by S.Z.

Homs governor standing nearby. Many of the people who used to pray were killed or have been forcibly displaced inside or outside Syria.

The Covered Souk in the Old City of Homs is another symbolic project that has been rehabilitated. Located at the heart of the city, the souk included over 1,000 shops before 2011, connecting the different parts of the city with one another. It was the most buzzing commercial hub in Homs, with its different branches such as al-A'tareen Souk (Perfumers' Souk). With its dark and solid cover, the souk created a sense of social cohesion where shopkeepers showed their products not only inside but also outside their shops. This all changed in 2011. The souks were at the heart of the destruction and shelling during the siege on the Old City. This led to the emergence of alternative shopping areas in other parts of Homs where streets have been turned into new markets, as in the Al Inshaat neighbourhood. Now, even though the Old City has been reopened, the souk area remains isolated as it is surrounded by ruined, desolate neighbourhoods. Many of the shopkeepers have been killed or displaced, whilst others prefer not to return to work there. The UNDP rehabilitated the souk with a team of local architects and engineers. The new cover of the souk looks different from the old one. It is open to the sky, so shops are not protected from the rain or the hot weather. Hence, even the ability to put their products outside their shops is limited, whilst the entire atmosphere of the cosy covered souk has changed. Many shopkeepers have started installing their own protection above their shops. UNHCR tents have been opened out and used to create an additional roof below the one the UNDP constructed.

The Syrian government uses the rehabilitation of cultural heritage sites for media purposes. There were hopes that reconstructing some of the iconic sites in Homs would be a blueprint to show that the city centre is reconstructing its pre-2011 life, but the residents in Homs tell me that the city centre is no longer the same, that the souk is no longer the busy heart of Homs. Several attempts have been made by the government to make people return to the souk and reopen their shops. In 2021, a member of the City Council of Homs issued an order giving shop owners a notice of two months to reopen and reinvest their shops in the old souk. Similar warnings were also issued in November 2020 by the Homs governor, who threatened to confiscate shops that failed to reopen (*The Syria Report* 2021a). But how can they be reopened when their owners are no longer there?

Whilst the rehabilitation of cultural heritage and symbolic sites is an essential part of the recovery of Homs, there are fears that cultural heritage sites will be used and abused. Rehabilitated sites such as the souks of Homs or Aleppo are often used in media platforms as propaganda that the current regime is the protector of the diverse communities and their cultural heritage. The rehabilitation of the Khalid ibn al-Walid Mosque was seen by many pro-government groups as a way to rebuild a place for the Sunni communities, whilst the rehabilitation of the Um Al Zennar Church was seen as a way to cement the idea that the regime protects Christians in Homs. These sites are also used and abused as ways to hide what happened to them, as if below the shiny facades and rehabilitated monuments, the struggle of Homs and its people is silenced. Such sites can be portrayed as pilot case studies to attract international funds and donations from governments and organizations interested in rebuilding cultural heritage after conflict. What is important to note is that reconstructing heritage can bury with it the stories of battles, violence and displacement. Acknowledging what happened to each of these sites should remain part of the healing process of local communities. Several cities have preserved parts of their ruins as sites for reflection and healing, including Berlin, Beirut, Hiroshima and Coventry. So, rather than burying the past and denying what happened, future reconstruction projects should enable a transparent and honest conversation about the motives behind reconstructing each site whilst engaging with local communities to remember the story of these sites.

During the years of conflict, the Syrian government has been keen to reconstruct memory and create new war heritage sites. Old destroyed monuments and statues have been rebuilt whilst new ones have emerged across the country (González Zarandona and Munawar 2020). These one-sided memorials that glorify the regime's narrative is an attempt to reconstruct identity. Through these memorials, the government enforces a one-dimensional narrative on the suffering and vulnerable communities. For instance, in October 2021, a memorial was inaugurated in Al Mukharram Alfuqaney in the eastern countryside of Homs, and in August 2019, a statue for the *Syrian Arabic Soldier* was inaugurated at the southern entrance of Homs. The statue shows a soldier opening his arms wide whilst holding the Syrian flag in his right hand. In April 2019, a memorial was inaugurated in the eastern countryside of Homs (Sulaiman 2019). The inauguration of memorials is often accompanied by the publication of articles and interviews about the event. These publications and videos also show the crowds, the celebrations, the dancing and the speeches as parts of such events. There are no memorials or public mourning allowed spatially in government-held areas for the civilians who were killed and families are left to mourn and grieve in silence.

Another memorial that was recently built in Homs is the Martyr's Monument in May 2019. It was called the Spirit of Basalt as it was made from basalt, stone that is used widely in the architecture of Homs. Online videos show crowds gathered for the opening, including the artist who designed the monument, and Talal Barazi, the mayor of Homs at the time. The monument emerged from the ruins of Old Homs in the shape of two arms holding up a soldier's helmet. The timing of the construction was announced by the Syrian government's media platforms as a way to mark the fifth year of the 'liberation' of Old Homs from 'terror', and also coincided with Martyrs' Day. Furthermore, it was the time when the government was announcing loudly and clearly that it had 'won' the war. The government used the materiality of the urban public spaces to glorify its achievements and silence the 'others' who believed in the revolution.

We need a critical analysis of the new memory sites in Syria. For this specific statue at the heart of Homs, different analytical lenses could be considered, including the timing of its construction and the choice of location. First, the timing was chosen when millions of people were still displaced from their homes and the war was (and is) still raging across the country. But it was an attempt to mark a turning point in time that Homs is a government-held city. Second, the location was carefully selected. The government did not build this memorial in one of its loyalist areas, but rather it chose a location that was the site of struggle and peaceful protests in early 2011. It is located in the Martyrs' Square, which is known by the Homsi communities as the Old Clock Square because it has a clock there which was built during the French Mandate. It is also on the same street that links with the New Clock Tower, which was the site of the Clock Massacre (see Chapter 2). In this square in Homs, protesters marched for the largest sit-in held in the heart of the city. So, to choose this site, is to tell those who revolted against the government that their dreams have been crushed and that they have no place for public mourning or remembering in the public space. Scholars researching different regions have pointed out the dangers of a one-sided history. As Bsheer says:

> Authorising state-sanctioned narratives and the spaces that materialize them are belligerent acts. Crafting and territorialising a singular history out of many entangled ones necessarily relies on the destruction, containment, and/or silencing of the evidentiary terrain[en] of people, places, and things. (2017: 129)

Each of the old or newly built memorials in Syria has its own story on why it was rehabilitated or built and why that particular location was chosen. The Old Clock Square has turned into a representation of the revolution in the past decade, and Homs itself has become known as the Capital of the Revolution. The government whitewashes this identity and erases the memory of the revolution from space. The materiality has an important aspect in the public realm through the physical presence of the memorial that goes beyond the bodily encounter. Places are witnesses of events and experiences that connect together. Places, therefore, are testimonies to events shaped by bombing, battles, destruction, decay and reconstruction (Viejo-Rose 2011). As the Old Clock Square marks the scars of wars and provides a testimony to the urban protests, the government is erasing this history from the place and is rewriting a new one.

The questions of cultural heritage sites have been of interest not only to the Syrian government but also to international audiences who poured in funds to debate Syria's heritage. In the past decade, many opinions have been written on Syria's cultural heritage sites by writers who know little about these sites. Who has the right to tell the story about Syria? And what story would they tell? When over half of the Syrian population has been displaced from their homes and over 90 per cent of the people are living in poverty, authors keep publishing about cultural heritage sites, not about the struggle of the people. In an article published in the *Guardian*, titled 'How Syria's Blasted Landmarks are Starting to Rise from the Ruins', Rowan Moore (2020) does not engage with any of the tens of local charities working on the ground or even with Syrian architects outside Syria who are pushing on different fronts to respond to the traumatic losses to their country. Rather, Moore highlights the work of organizations in Berlin and Geneva. Such an example in one of the most read newspapers in the UK and beyond shows how writers can be selective on who to write about, and hence, who to put under the spotlight as if they are our guardians, the ones saving our own heritage. When reading the article, I wondered if the *Guardian* would publish pieces by someone who knows about the local work on the ground, or at least ask one of the tens of Syrian architects to contribute or bring their voices to the piece?

Particularly monumental and ancient heritage has captured a global attention whilst neglecting the suffering and pain of people. Palmyra is perhaps one of these remarkable sites that has been covered widely in the media when it was attacked by ISIS in 2015. This led to the proliferation of almost an entire 'industry' and networks on protecting heritage and reconstructing it. At the Institute for Digital Archaeology (IDA), for instance, a replica of Palmyra's Arch was 3D-printed and exhibited at different sites. The replica, which is two-thirds the original scale of the arch, was first exhibited in Trafalgar Square in London. The homepage of the IDA's website (accessed in February 2021), features the replica of the Arch of Palmyra in Trafalgar Square as the first image one can see there. But for whom is this replica? The image on the landing webpage of the IDA shows how cultural heritage has been used through political dimensions. One photo on the landing webpage of the IDA shows Roger Michel, the institute's founder and executive director, and Boris Johnson, Loncon's mayor at the time, standing by the replica. In another photo, Michel is the central figure standing between Sheikh Mohammed bin Rashid Al Maktoum, prime minister of the United Arab Emirates and Emir of Dubai, and Irina Bokova, the former director-general of UNESCO. What messages do these images send? During a presentation once, I asked attendees to log into the IDA's website and report back what they see and what messages they read when looking at these images. Some responses included: white saviour, old white men, commoditizing culture, framing of empire, politics and monument parallelisms.

Watching these images shows the powers shaping the questions of reconstruction, the politics involved and the 'use' of our cultural heritage sites to rewrite another narrative. I wondered where the Syrians were in these pictures. I could not spot them, but it seems that Michel did. In a short piece published by the *New York Times*, he talks about his interests and explains what he is reading, listening to and watching (Murphy 2016). In the watching section, he said he had been sitting in Trafalgar Square watching people who came to touch and feel the arch, including 'Syrians in traditional dress.' I have met hundreds of Syrians in the UK, and I do not know what he means by that. This emphasis on celebrity-like monuments and sites have overshadowed the questions surrounding the loss of people's homes and their sense of belonging in the neighbourhoods. I bring these examples here because there are fears that future reconstruction will be a continuation of these projects. Mosques, temples, churches and ancient sites will be reconstructed, but not people's homes, not their everyday urban, social and cultural fabrics, and not their lesser-known places.

Conclusions

Emerging debates on the future reconstruction in Syria can be divided into two main themes, first the construction of mega-residential projects for the rich and elite (e.g. Marota City), and second the protection and reconstruction of cultural heritage sites. Little research and architectural efforts have been directed towards thinking about reconstruction as a housing project for the millions of people who lost their homes and have been displaced. The Syrian government is using and abusing heritage for history writing and rewriting. Through the construction of new heritage sites in Syria as memorials, statues, a singular history narrative is imposed to dictate and curate the future. Heritage can be seen then as a violent process, and a continuation of narrative wars.

Whilst many studies on conflict and the city have focused on 'post-war' and 'post-conflict' reconstruction (Bullock 2002; Grodach 2002; Aita 2020), I intended in this section to highlight the 'wartime' debates on reconstruction. This body of work has been hugely absent in the growing research on conflicts and cities. Conflicts are not only radically changing cities around the world, but they themselves are changing, too (Kaldor and Sassen, 2020). Increasingly, we are witnessing countries going through long-term conflicts, and in many cases, the conflict dynamics constantly change. Even years since the start of the revolution, Syria remains divided and contested. So, rather than waiting for a 'post-war' reconstruction, it is important today to research the wartime conversations by Syrian refugees and migrants.

As I mentioned in the introduction of this chapter, scholars focusing on different war-torn geographies have debated the fears and anxieties associated with reconstruction that bring with them new landscapes of loss, domicide and destructions (Hubbard, Faire and Lilley 2003; Viejo-Rose 2011; Webb 2018). Whilst destruction is mostly associated with periods of violence and urban conflicts, these studies demonstrate how reconstruction can cause more destruction in the aftermath of wars, in times of 'peace'. In different geographies across the world, cities have lost much of their architecture and heritage in the time of 'peace' following the end of civil wars, conflicts and periods of violence. In Lebanon, after the end of the Civil War of 1975–90, Beirut's city centre was reconstructed with an attempt to bury and deny the country's years of war through creating a 'forgetful landscape' (Nagel 2002: 723). Buildings were knocked down in the city centre, paving the way for a new image of the heart of Beirut, that disoriented Beirutis. During this process, over three-quarters of the still-standing buildings in the city centre at the end of the war were demolished in the first phase of reconstruction (Badescu 2011). Hashim Sarkis (2006: 286) notes that this clearing of the downtown created a 'collective homesickness for Beirutis even if they still resided in Beirut'. This reconstructed city centre, mainly led by Solidere, has often attracted tourists and foreign visitors, whilst many members of the local communities have felt excluded from being there, from reclaiming their city centre.

Architecture and urban planning have been used as tools for repeated damage and harm on vulnerable communities who lost their homes in the time of war and peace. Domicidal plans emerge in the name of 'redevelopment' and 'reconstruction'. In Syria, when conflict frontlines have been shifting across the country, destroying people's homes, another war was taking place in the name of redevelopment and urbanization with bulldozers erasing neighbourhoods. Neighbourhoods in Hama and Damascus, for instance, were demolished because they were 'informal' or 'illegal', or because these areas were valuable and needed to be 'redeveloped'. Political and economic powers use these projects as a vacuum for capital to benefit the rich but cause more suffering and harm to the poor, leading to mass homelessness and deep suffering to their dwellers. These luxurious projects are launched and promoted to attract local and foreign millionaires and investors, raising key questions about class dimensions and rights to the city.

For whom is the reconstruction? For whom are these projects? Will the millions of refugees who have been uprooted from their homes have the right to live in these projects? Those who live across the world in countries such as Türkiye, Jordan, Lebanon, Germany and the UK, will they have the right to return? And if they have lost their home, will their home be reconstructed for them? The millions of IDPs who suffered from multiple displacements and extreme levels of poverty, will they be allowed to live in these new reconstruction projects? Or do they not fit in with the 'modern' citizen who should be living in these 'modern' neighbourhoods? Are reconstruction projects solely targeted at the rich? Or will there be housing projects that prioritize impacted communities and the poor who have lost so much during the past decade? Will communities have the right to reclaim their built environment and shape the future of their towns and villages, or will they be excluded, silenced and unheard? These are some of the questions that should be linked to any reconstruction project today.

For those who do not know that these shiny projects are built on the misery of the poor and on lands soaked with blood, such projects might be seen as if Syria is being reconstructed again, 'rising from the ashes'. They might be applauded and perhaps supported by those who are distant from the daily struggle of Syrians and lack the understanding of the Syrian context. Indeed, politicians and property developers can use reconstruction as a propaganda tool to hide the misery and struggle of millions of people. Shiny glass towers offering a lavish lifestyle and expensive cars in exclusive gated neighbourhoods are proposed and might be shown to the world as a blueprint for future reconstructions. Fears and anxieties are now emerging from future imagined towns and cities, from violence that will manifest itself through space, through displacing people and pushing them from their homes, through new waves of domicide, through rebuilding for the few whilst those vulnerable communities are left in a life without any form of support to rebuild their ruined lives.

5

Domicide in war and peace

'We are still here'

On 15 March 2021, Mona Rafea (pseudonym) reflected on the tenth anniversary of the Syrian uprising in an article titled, 'We're Still Here' (2021). Writing from inside Homs, the Capital of the Revolution, Rafea has provided a rare reflection on the urban life in the city, taking readers to places and spaces of everydayness. Publishing from within Homs, or undertaking any type of activism, has been very rare in the past decade due to security reasons. Any article or critique about the current situation could lead to arrest.

The title of Rafea's article is a statement in itself. 'We're still here' is a statement about the presence of the people who remain in Homs despite the displacement of over half of Syria's population, and despite the disappearance of Homs from the news headlines. After twelve years of struggle, Homs and Syria have gradually faded away from the public consciousness, whilst the pain of the people continues silently. It is also a statement about the need to remember the revolution in order not to forget. As millions of Syrians have found refuge in exile, the bridge between those inside and outside Syria continues to lengthen. The voice of Rafea, therefore, and the stories she has documented, have become windows on Homs for people who have been displaced from the city. Although Rafea writes about the collective sense of loss in Homs, and the collapse of the way of life there, she remains persistent in keeping hope in her writing, to show that the struggle and resistance continue, even if only inside the hearts of the people rather than being practised publicly in their protests as they did in the past. As she notes:

> We're still here, in Homs. There is still a firmness within us. We walk, and sleep, and eat, and fear, and dream. What matters is that we still dream. The one thing we are still certain of is that no one can uproot what is in our hearts, no matter how much the opposite may appear to be the case. (Rafea 2021)

Two years before this article was published, she wrote about 'Spaces of Masculinity', describing how Homs transformed into a city mostly of women, children, the elderly, *shabiha* (state-sponsored militias for the Syrian Government) and young men who are fearful to be taken into military service and who plan to leave the country during the second or third year of their university studies. She referred to the displacement of men from the country and the changing roles of women in Homs. In 'Spaces of Masculinity', she dealt with questions of sex and gender and noted that she wishes to be a man, to have a hoarse voice that she could use to shout at the regime's military men. By this imagination, she wants to resist. She notes:

> I want to scream in their faces. I want to scream in the faces of everyone, everyyyyyone, with my hoarse voice, instead of the silent crying, instead of the repeated pain of the soul, instead of complaining about powerlessness and helplessness, instead of succumbing to despair that has made me like an invisible desperate ghost. (Rafea 2019)

Rafea refuses to remain hopeless even when living in a city of oppression and injustice. She describes this sense of being invisible in 'Spaces of Masculinity'. Her writing is an act to resist the wiping-out of people, their history, the demolition of their homes and the burning of their belongings and documents. Rafea refuses to remain powerless, even if her power and the power of the people of Homs is only kept in their hearts. Through her writings, she imagines whole new worlds where she can fight this sense of powerlessness, where she can shout at the military men in a form of rebellion. Beyond her imagination, Rafea has already rebelled. She has already fought back through the writings she has produced, with all the risks that she has been taking to write from within Homs, unlike many who remain silent and fearful until today even when they are outside of the country.

There are many reasons that make the work of Rafea significant. One of these reasons is her ability to make the everyday life in Homs accessible to those who are no longer able to return to visit their city. By doing so, she makes the invisible visible through her writing. Rob Nixon, the author of 'Slow Violence and the Environmentalism of the Poor', explains the power of writing. As he notes (2011: 15), 'in a world permeated by insidious, yet unseen or imperceptible violence, imaginative writing can help make the unapparent appear, making it accessible and tangible by humanizing drawn-out threats inaccessible to the immediate senses'. This is what Rafea has been doing in her writing. The narrative of writer-activists, as Nixon puts it, may 'offer us a different kind of witnessing: of sights unseen'. Outside Syria, Rafea is now widely read, and celebrated as an anonymous author who makes the unseen seen through her words. In 2022, the Celebrating Syria Festival in Manchester and *Al Jumhuriya*, the magazine that published Rafea's work, put together an event as a tribute to celebrate her work and share her writings with international audiences.

We stand today on the ruins of a world that once was. We are living daily the rupture of history. After more than a decade since the start of the Syrian Revolution, many are losing hope that change is still possible. Others are feeling powerless in the face of the individual and collective trauma. This is why it is important to reconstruct hope, and to search for old, new and existing tools and devices to resist domicide. In *Hope in the Dark: Untold Histories, Wild Possibilities*, Rebecca Solnit (2016) makes a radical case for hope in a world shaped by uncertainties, pessimism, despair and unimaginable futures yet to come. She says that her writing is meant to give aid and comfort to people overwhelmed by the defeatist perspective and to encourage people to stand up, to participate, to look forward to what we can do collectively and back at what we have done. Memory is essential for her in reconstructing hope. She even makes an analogy that if the branches are of hope, then the roots are memory. In other words, whilst hope is about imagining the future, the grounds for this hope lie in the records and recollections of the past. I return to *Hope in the Dark* in search of the radical questions that we need to ask in the Syrian context today, and I build on Solnit's case of hope and memory as tools to fight amnesia and despair, and to find new springs of optimism in dark times. As Solnit puts it (2016: xi):

> Your opponents would love you to believe that it's hopeless, that you have no power, that there's no reason to act, that you can't win. Hope is a gift you don't have to surrender, a power you don't have to throw away.

In the following section, I offer some recommendations and suggestions for resisting domicide.

Resisting domicide: Reclaiming our narrative

Domicide sufferers and victims are often seen by those who destroy their homes as unaccountable, subhuman or wasted: they have no place and should be removed from their society. The destruction of their homes goes hand in hand with silencing their voices. When we hear about the destruction of homes, we rarely hear the voices of impacted people. This lack of representation has raised many ethical and moral questions about conducting research on conflicts and domicide (Zhang 2014; Abdelnour and Abu Moghli 2021).

Very often the stories of impacted communities and refugees are unheard in big conferences and events. In 2017, a conference in Oxford was organized on refugee studies, with tens of attendees and speakers. One of the papers presented at the conference reviewed the several proposals that call for 'refugee islands' such as a 'Europe-in-Africa' city-state on the Tunisian Plateau that was proposed by a Dutch architect. The speaker moved further to present the work he did on imagining a place that is governed by the refugees themselves. During the questions-and-answers session, a man raised his hand to comment. The mic was given to him and his voice could be heard throughout the conference room which was very large. He angrily started telling the speaker that he knows nothing about the struggle of the refugees and that he is disconnected from the harsh reality of the forcibly displaced people. He used the 'f' word on the speaker and then started crying. This was one of the many times I have seen the disappointment of impacted communities on how their struggle is being transformed into imagined fantasies, how their narrative is taken from them. In another international conference in London in the same year, I attended a presentation on Aleppo. The woman sitting next to me, whom I did not know, looked at me in the middle of the presentation and said, 'this woman knows nothing about Aleppo', in reference to the presenter. After that, she left the event whilst the speaker was still presenting. In any research on conflict and cities, we need to ask what is the knowledge produced for? What are the right research questions to ask about conflict studies? By whom and for whom? Are the questions relevant? Can they lead to a radical change in the face of suffering?

There are many people today standing in solidarity with Syrians and keeping Syria at the heart of their work. They are creating platforms to engage with impacted communities, establishing meaningful programmes that are led and/or co-designed with the Syrian people, and calling for inclusive recruitment across different sectors to hire refugees. These foundations of solidarity have been of great importance in the past twelve years. However, the critique that I provide in the following paragraphs should not be understood as a concern for dividing along national lines. Rather, I hope this critique will be understood as an encouragement to rethink the way in which we deal with the pain of others, and the ways aid, care, solidarity and support are practised.

Many international humanitarian aid workers have seen in the Syrian crisis an opportunity to live in cosmopolitan cities with a high income that privileges them over the local communities in the countries where they work. Amman and Beirut have been amongst these cities that attracted aid workers from across the world who have been privileged to study in elitist universities, and then work in the most powerful and richest institutions that pay them far more than the local people. Chatty (2017) wrote about the presence of these aid workers in such cities that have encouraged the development of a kind of 'aid tourism'. She expands further to explain how these international aid workers deal with displaced Syrians, whom they are supposed to be serving, as being of secondary importance in their day-to-day lives. Chatty also notes how local NGOs complain as they feel they are officially 'labelled' as partners with these international organizations, but their voices and experiences are often ignored whilst their services are seen as low level. This reflects the tension between local and international powers. I present this example here because many Syrians feel that their voices are unheard by those Syria 'experts' who study and work at top universities and live privileged lifestyles. Many of the scholars working on Syria are alienated from Syrians and their suffering but see in our pain and trauma a way to progress in their careers.

For many academics and researchers, and those working in the humanitarian and charity sector, Syria has become a funding opportunity. In 2019, at the University of Cambridge, an academic said to me that I am a great funding opportunity for researchers. At the same university, I also attended a panel discussion on Syria with four speakers and a chair. None of them was Syrian. A UK-based academic said to me that Syria is an attractive and fashionable conflict site when compared to other countries such as Yemen and Libya. According to her, many scholars in the 'West' see in the cultural heritage sites in Syria a link to them, as if it is their own heritage. I cannot recall the number of times I have been contacted by architecture students doing their Master's thesis or developing their PhDs on Syria, or academics who are applying for funds asking for support in their applications but without any meaningful engagement. Sometimes I was simply contacted with a request to connect them with other people. On one occasion, an academic reached out to me just before the submission of his funding application, asking me to write a support letter for his work. I did not know the person to examine the quality of his work and his views on the Syrian context. He explained in the email that he was focusing on a site in Syria that he never visited and literally knew nothing about. Our pain is becoming the funding opportunity for those who know little about the trauma we have been through. After more than a decade of loss, trauma and destruction, it felt many times that our narrative has been lost too, that it has been shaped by people with different competing agendas. Scholars, think tanks and NGOs have made our suffering an opportunity for their careers.

We are interesting to them simply because we are their next funding opportunity. Once Syria is not fundable, they jump onto another suffering community – now Ukraine. So, our bodies and our stories are their projects. So, they wrote about us. They spoke about us. They discussed us. They filmed us. They presented us. They represented us. They are interested in the tents we lived in. In the video calls we had with our families. They collected money in our names. They won funds in our names. They got new positions. They were promoted for their achievements. They are the ones who saved us and saved our heritage. They are celebrated for how they changed our ruined lives and how they preserved our own heritage. They applied for awards that were created for them and for people similar to them who went to the best universities and best institutions and have the best and strongest connections. They received awards that should have been given to the impacted communities and the people who suffered the most, to the people who fought every day for survival and who supported one another with limited resources and vulnerable environments. But these awards do not find their way to impacted communities. We have turned into a fundable project for academics, and the best-winning article chance for journalists. They photographed themselves with replicas of our heritage. They photographed themselves with Syria's children in refugee camps. But few of them knew what it means to live in a world without a stable centre, to live the rupture of history, to lose one's home and homeland.

If they invite us to join them at the same table, then perhaps it is the time for them to take photographs and show how 'engaged' they are with Syrian voices. How many times have we attended a panel discussion or an event on Syria with no Syrian on the panel? It felt like International Women's Day with all-men in panels – manels. All these frustrations and dilemmas have made me write about our right to reclaim our narrative. So, I sat down one day in 2020, and published a thread on Twitter which has been viewed over 700,000 times, with thousands of people across the world commenting on it and sharing it. In parts of the thread, I noted:

> As a Syrian in the UK, I've seen how some UK based academics turned our pain & trauma into an opportunity for them, who saw in us a funding opportunity. Many of them wouldn't speak the language, know our struggle, or care about us, but hey, it's good for their career? [thread]
>
> This has been often the case in almost an industry like field on Syria's heritage. Suddenly everyone wants to write about Palmyra, even those who never visited, or met a Syrian in their lives, whilst they would neglect the struggle of people whose lives have been damaged.

We need to raise ethical questions about work on conflicts. When I published the thread online, researchers, activists and academics around the world noted that this is not the case for Syria, but for countries such as Lebanon, Sudan, Palestine, Bosnia and Mexico. It is important for those working on conflict zones to be trained on how to conduct their research ethically. Even those who might have 'good intentions' might cause harm if they come with their own predesigned programmes without listening to, or meaningfully engaging with, impacted communities.

Collective spaces of solidarity

There is a need for creating inclusive spaces of solidarity for Syrians working in the built environment domain. These spaces can be physical in local areas, digital platforms connecting people remotely or hybrid where people can work together across different regions. Although the past decade has witnessed the emergence of work by Syrian architects, urban planners, writers and academics, these efforts remain largely disconnected and scattered. Creating collective spaces of support and solidarity will help to exchange knowledge, foster collaboration and learn from one another. Throughout history, such spaces have been established at the time of war. During the Second World War, the Polish School of Architecture was inaugurated at the University of Liverpool in November 1942. The British Council at the time approached the university with the proposal. The school offered a space for staff and students to work on theoretical schemes such as the rebuilding of residential blocks and town halls.

Today, different initiatives and programmes can be proposed in the case of Syria, as well as other contested regions such as Iraq, Yemen and Libya. Some of these initiatives can include:

1. Organizing workshops that explore different themes around the built environment in Syria, e.g. reconstruction, participatory planning, cultural heritage and rehabilitation. It would be great to organize a series of workshops that are sustainable and repeatable in the long term rather than being designed for short-term purposes. The continuation and repetition of these workshops would help to enhance collaborations and create stronger relationships between partners and organizations.

2. Establishing writing programmes where Syrian architects at different stages of their career can join writing groups and publish their work individually or as a collective. Such programmes must ensure that different voices are represented from different parts of Syria. Most of the emerging writing on Syria's built environment is focused on Damascus or Aleppo, and architects from other cities such as Idlib, Raqqa, Hama and Al Hasaka should be included and offered spaces to participate. An example of a writing platform on cities (though not focused on Syria only), is the Arab Urbanism, which focuses on the

past, present and future of cities in the Arab region. It was established in 2020, with contributions published both in Arabic and English.

3. Creating mentorship programmes where architects who have work experience can offer support to university students. This could be applied to architects who are based inside or outside Syria, and architects could be matched based on their level of experience and research interests. Mentors can be from Syria or from another nationality, depending on the wants and needs of the mentees. These programmes can be established within architectural practices in the private sector, from within academic institutions or through NGOs that build bridges between different organizations and Syrian architects.

4. Co-establishing and co-leading research projects on different aspects of the built environment. This would be beneficial to Syrian architects outside Syria as they have limited access to information and resources on the ground. It is also beneficial to architects inside Syria as they can be connected with those outside the country who have access to different networks, funding programmes and publications.

The creation of such spaces will be facing several challenges. One of these challenges is the divisions across Syrians themselves. Many Syrian architects who are working on Syria still refuse to talk to one another due to the political divide. In the UK, there are architects who used to work together or be colleagues at the same university inside Syria before the revolution but now no longer talk to each other. How would an architect accept talking to someone who reported them for supporting the revolution? How can someone who lost family members at the hands of the Syrian government talk and collaborate with someone who supports the government? Is there a chance to create 'grey zones' between different groups with all the dividing lines? Would there be a way to make a change from an architecture point of view even if no political change was achieved?

There is another level of divide that continues to separate Syrians from one another. It is the divide between those who remain inside Syria and those who left the country. How can we create collective spaces that connect these groups of people together? What forms should these spaces take? And would it be possible to rebuild trust between divided communities? Many of the architects who are working on Syria projects are refugees who have not been back to Syria since they left the country – this might be a decade or more for some people – others might be of Syrian origin who were raised abroad but have never lived in Syria. Some of those who have Syrian heritage but have never lived in Syria feel they are excluded or questioned about their positionality when they work on Syria. It is therefore important to work collectively whilst acknowledging differences and the experiences, motives, knowledge and aspirations of these different groups.

For those who fled Syria after the war, understanding the everyday life inside the country is limited due to the lack of connection with local communities who remain in war-torn cities and villages. Architects in diaspora, therefore, might be relying only on their own experiences and knowledge before leaving the country, or on the emerging reports of local and international organizations. Whilst they might be working and collaborating with other Syrians in exile, their challenge is to co-create knowledge with and for local communities inside the country – in case their projects are focused on areas inside Syria rather than on the questions of refuge and exile. Building bridges between those inside and outside of Syria is crucial as the gap keeps widening, impacting the type and quality of knowledge being produced on Syria and raising questions about why and for whom this knowledge is being produced. Many of the architects outside Syria are researching the politics of reconstruction and the weaponization of the built environment. There is a high level of risk to research such topics within the government-held areas in Syria because of the current political climate. Any collaborations with people inside government-held areas, therefore, need to be carefully designed and conducted in a way that protects the safety of the participants and respects their situation. Another factor that impacts the dynamics of collaboration between architects within and outside Syria is related to funds. Those outside Syria might have access to funds to cover their time and conduct their projects. Several funding institutions and universities do not allow any funds to be transferred to collaborators inside Syria due to economic sanctions on the country. This leads to unequal access to financial support and leaves those inside Syria without any funds in these projects.

As a way to bridge the gap between architects inside and outside Syria, digital platforms can offer an opportunity to exchange knowledge and connect people together. Wesam Al Asali, for instance, established Urbegony: Architecture, Education, Without Borders, Syria, in 2015. Urbegony is an online education platform that works with architecture students in different cities in Syria. Al Asali's work has been conducted remotely as he lives outside Syria. Online networks have been embraced by several communities impacted by conflicts and wars. In 2021, the Iraqi Women Academics Network (IWAN) was established as a platform with a global reach, supporting women academics inside and outside Iraq. More of these networks are needed today across different contested and divided regions and across different disciplines not limited to architecture. Today, we are living in a critical moment of history where cities have been radically reshaped by wars across different countries in the past decade and where millions of people are forcibly displaced from their countries but remain longing to connect with their homes. The establishment of collective networks can act as a foundation of solidarity to give people hope in the dark, to inspire a sense of agency and a sense of hope that we can shape our own history.

Protecting memory

The mass destruction of architecture in Syria, the loss of people's homes, the restrictions of freedoms and the radical erasure of the sources of the material history, have all led to a new area of inquiry, to an entirely new typology: the study of memory. Since 2011, a new body of work has emerged about tracing the past of Syria at times when villages, towns and cities have been turned into ruins. The work of activists, archivists, academics, artists like Deanna Petherbridge and writers such as Mona Rafea have all contributed to the exploration of imagined and destroyed homelands. As we mark more than a decade since the start of the revolution in Syria, we must protect memory.

The protection of memory should be central to the struggle of Syria and Syrians when both tangible and intangible history have been wilfully targeted and contested. This centralization of memory should also influence the future reconstruction process to capture the rhythms of longing for erased pasts. By exploring the relationship between reconstruction and memory, many questions should be considered: how could the reconstruction of the built environment recreate a sense of belonging in the aftermath of the war? How much to remember? And how much to forget? How could architects preserve a continuation of the pre-war memory whilst at the same time improve the living conditions of people? What pieces of history should be reconstructed and recreated? There are neighbourhoods that have been completely razed to the ground since 2011, and some of the emerging reconstruction plans propose further destruction of cities, including the removal of still-standing buildings. Memory is not only destroyed in time of war, but also in the time of 'peace' in the name of reconstruction, regeneration or modernization.

As a response to domicide and the destructive reconstruction projects, architects, artists and historians are renegotiating their past and reconstructing the memory of their villages and cities. They work on restoring the identity and cultural heritage of their erased built environment. This interest in reconstructing memory has led to the creation of tens of social media pages to remember, for example the Museum of Homs City's Old Photos and the Forum Studying the History of Homs. Images of different parts of the city have re-emerged amongst people who are nostalgic for their lost city and what it looked like in the past. Even spaces of ordinary everyday life, of small houses, doors or windows and of strait alleyways have become cherished, more precious and increasingly popular.

Violence at home

In this book, I have attempted to reconstruct the notion of domicide by bringing the destruction of the built environment closer to the suffering of impacted communities within the Syrian context. By doing so, I have preferred not to focus exclusively on the destruction of the tangible and material history. Rather, I wanted to bring the voices of impacted communities to the centre of thinking about violence and the built environment. I argued that narrowly focusing on the destruction of architecture is inadequate to understand what it means to lose home, and what it means to be dispossessed from one's own home. Therefore, the experiences of the victims of domicide need to be at the centre of the current debates on violence and domicide, and at the heart of the future reconstruction of Syria. Until now, and despite the mass destruction of people's homes, their voices are often unheard or not listened to. The future reconstruction should not only focus on building for the people but also *with* the people. By doing so, the reconstruction project can enhance a sense of agency where people feel they belong, they count, their voices are heard.

By taking domicide as a theoretical frame, I focus on the social suffering of people impacted by the destruction of home. I build on the narratives of longing, loss, grief, nostalgia and suffering of the victims of violence. These narratives of people inside and outside Syria shed light on the symbolic and material impact of domicide in the process of making, unmaking and remaking home. Oral accounts of people interviewed in this research show that symbolic violence is at the centre of domicide as they feel not only that their homes are being destroyed, but also that their own presence in Syria is threatened. The destruction of people's homes meant an assault on their dignity, identity and sense of belonging.

Another point that has been highlighted in this book is the link between violence at the time of war and peace. Before the start of the revolution, violence segregated communities from one another and destroyed the tangible history spatially in the name of modernization and development. Violence has taken more extreme forms since the start of the revolution. Now, as 'post-war' reconstruction plans emerge, there are fears that domicide will continue to manifest itself during the time of 'peace'. In *For the War Yet to Come*, Hiba Bou Akar (2019: 177) makes the case for examining the link between war and peace violence in Beirut, Lebanon. She argues that 'in Beirut's peripheries, war and peace, arrested development and growth, coexistence and segregation, destruction and construction, home and displacement are intimately entangled'. More than three decades after the end of the Civil War in Lebanon, the cycles of violence and displacement continue to 'redefine otherness and engender new forms and mechanisms of spatial segregation'. By understanding this link between violence in the time of war and peace, we can see that the end of the battlefields is not the end of social suffering. So, what can we learn from the past? How can reconstruction be built on justice, social cohesion, inclusivity and sustainability? How can we avoid a future in ruins?

A final point I wish to note is what Yunpeng Zhang (2018: 209) refers to as the belated nature of domicide effects. At the time of writing this book, over half of the Syrian population remains displaced and villages, towns and cities remain in ruins. The grief that people have narrated personally should also be seen as part of a wider collective trauma of the Syrian people. This grief and trauma of domicide will continue as people long for their lost home and homeland, and as they struggle with identity crises, the disappearance of the support network around them and the pain of separation from the places and people they have left. Hence, the impact of domicide continues throughout the lifetime of its victims who retell and relive their story and trauma. Some people have told me that they keep seeing themselves as having returned to Syria in their dreams, but that even in the dream they were fearing arrest and violence. This is why Zhang argues that we must understand the effects of domicide as 'constantly unfolding and incomplete'. The impact of war, destruction and displacement is not limited to the moment of violence. It does not end at the time of reaching a new country. For impacted communities, the struggle continues slowly, daily, it manifests itself temporally through the lens of time, when everyday life in itself becomes a war of its own.

Bibliography

Abaza, M. (2011), 'Critical Commentary. Cairo's Downtown Imagined: Dubaisation or Nostalgia?', *Urban Studies*, 48 (6): 1075–87. doi: 10.1177/0042098011399598.

Abdelnour, S. and M. Abu Moghli (2021), 'Researching Violent Contexts: A Call for Political Reflexivity', *Organization*. doi: 10.1177/13505084211030646.

Aboelezz, M. (2015), 'The Geosemiotics of Tahrir Square: A Study of the Relationship between Discourse and Space', *Journal of Language and Politics*, 13 (4). doi: 10.1075/jlp.13.4.02abo.

Abou Zainedin, S. (2019), 'Weaponised Urbanism', *aljumhuriya*. Available online: https://www.aljumhuriya.net/ar/topics/عسكرة_العمران (accessed 26 December 2022).

Abujidi, N. (2014), *Urbicide in Palestine: Spaces of Oppression and Resilience*, Abingdon: Routledge. doi: 10.4324/9781315819099.

Achcar, G. (2013), *The People Want: A Radical Exploration of the Arab Uprising*, London: Saqi Books. doi: 10.5860/choice.51-6393.

Aita, S. (2020), *Urban Recovery Framework for Post-Conflict Housing in Syria*, Paris: Samir Aita and the Cercle des Economistes Arabes. Available online: http://www.economistes-arabes.org/fr/urban-recovery-framework-for-post-conflict-housing-in-syria/ (accessed 26 December 2022).

Akesson, B., A. R. Basso and M. Denov (2016), 'The Right to Home: Domicide as a Violation of Child and Family Rights in the Context of Political Violence', in *Children and Society*, 30 (5). doi: 10.1111/chso.12174.

Aks Alser (2007), 'The "Homs Dream" Causes Protests and Denunciations in the Public Opinion in the City', *Aks Alser*. Available online: https://aksalser.com/?page=view_articles&id=c40f6741971b77661602570541f4dbfc (accessed 26 December 2022).

Al Arabiya (2019), *Al Awamiyah's Centre: The Prince of the Eastern Region Reveals to Al Arabiya the Details of the Project*, video, YouTube, 6 January. Available online: https://www.youtube.com/watch?v=gXVzDO3zrj4 (accessed 24 December 2022).

Al Asali, M. W. (2020), 'Craftsmanship for Reconstruction: Artisans Shaping Syrian Cities', in F. Arefian and S. Moeini (eds), *Urban Heritage Along the Silk Roads*, Urban Book Series, 107–19, Cham: Springer. doi: 10.1007/978-3-030-22762-3_8.

Al Masri, E. (2013), 'The Rehabilitation of Urban Environment in Homs Old City – Syria: "An Opinion and an Experiment"', Damascus: University of Damascus.

Al Masri, E. and H. Al Sajaz (n.d.), *'Considerations of Doing and Rehabilitation to the Strategic Plans': Study Homs City*. Available online: https://360doc.files.wordpress.com/2011/04/d8a7d8b9d8aad8a8d8a7d8b1d8a7d8aa.pdf (accessed 26 December 2022).

BIBLIOGRAPHY

al-Haj Saleh, Y. (2017), *The Impossible Revolution: Making Sense of the Syrian Tragedy*, London: Hurst.

Al-Homsi, A. (2013), 'Burning the City Council in Homs between the Opposition's Claim and the Regime's Denial', *Enab Baladi*. Available at: https://www.enabbaladi.net/archives/9476 (accessed 26 December 2022).

Al-Jazaeri, R. (2019), 'Xiaodong: China Will Continue to Support and Cooperate with Syria in Combating Terrorism', *SANA*. Available online: https://sana.sy/en/?p=180348 (accessed 26 December 2022).

Al-Kateab, W. and E. Watts (2019), *For Sama*, film, London: Channel 4 News / ITN Productions.

Al-Sabouni, M. (2016), *The Battle for Home: Memoir of a Syrian Architect*, London: Thames & Hudson.

Al-Sabouni, M. (2021), *Building for Hope: Towards an Architecture of Belonging*, London: Thames & Hudson. Available online: https://thamesandhudson.com.au/product/building-for-hope-towards-an-architecture-of-belonging/ (accessed 26 December 2022).

Aljaml (2007), *Between the Officials and Brokers, the Homs Dream Crawls over the Dreams of the PoorLlike Centipedes, aljaml*. Available online: https://www.aljaml.com/ما‌بين‌المسؤولين‌والسماسرة‌حلم‌حمص‌يزحف‌على‌أحلام‌الفقراء‌كأم 44 (accessed 30 January 2022).

Allen, K. (2019), 'Raqqa is in Ruins Like a Modern Dresden: This is Not "Precision Bombing"', *Guardian*, 23 May. Available online: https://www.theguardian.com/commentisfree/2019/may/23/raqqa-ruins-bombing (accessed 26 December 2022).

Amnesty International (2015), '"We Had Nowhere Else to Go": Forced Displacement and Demolitions in Northern Syria'. Available online: https://www.amnesty.org/download/Documents/MDE2425032015ENGLISH.PDF (accessed 26 December 2022).

Amnesty International (2019), *The Ruins of Liberation*. Available online: https://player.slices.co/stories/-LbYHjqML6BqMbZW6njy?canonicalUrl=amnesty.nl/raqqa (accessed 26 December 2022).

Arab News (2018), 'Luxury Marota City Project Shows Blueprint for Syria's Rebuilding Plans'. Available online: https://www.arabnews.com/node/1399411/middle-east (accessed 26 December 2022).

Arab Reform Initiative (2015), *Tahdir for Syria*. Available online: https://www.arab-reform.net/project/tahdir-for-syria/ (accessed 26 December 2022).

Atkinson, R. (2015), 'Losing One's Place: Narratives of Neighbourhood Change, Market Injustice and Symbolic Displacement', *Housing, Theory and Society*, 32 (4): 373–88.

Azzouz, A. (2018), 'Architects at the Time of War', Royal Institute of British Architects. Available online: https://www.architecture.com/awards-and-competitions-landing-page/awards/riba-presidents-awards-for-research/2018/architects-at-the-time-of-war (accessed 26 December 2022).

Azzouz, A. (2019), 'A Tale of a Syrian City at War: Destruction, Resilience and Memory in Homs', *City*, 23 (1): 107–22. doi: 10.1080/13604813.2019.1575605.

Azzouz, A. (2020a), '"I Can Smell Aleppo": Waad Al-Kateab Shows Us a City Under Siege', *City*, 23 (6): 792–7. doi: 10.1080/13604813.2020.1719762.

Azzouz, A. (2020b), 'Re-imagining Syria: Destructive Reconstruction and the Exclusive Rebuilding of Cities', *City*, 24 (5–6): 721–40. doi: https://doi.org/10.1080/13604813.2020.1833536.

Azzouz, A. (2020c), 'Re-imagining Syria: On Memory and Memoricide', *City*, 24 (5–6).: 721–40 doi.org/10.1080/13604813.2020.1833536.

Azzouz, A. (2022), 'Our Pain, Their Heritage Project: From the Palmyra Moment to Violence and the City', *Change Over Time*, 11 (2): 162–80.

Baban, F., S. Ilcan and K. Rygiel (2017), 'Syrian Refugees in Turkey: Pathways to Precarity, Differential Inclusion, and Negotiated Citizenship Rights', *Journal of Ethnic and Migration Studies*, 43 (1): 41–57. doi: 10.1080/1369183X.2016.1192996.

Badescu, G. (2011), 'Beyond the Green Line: Sustainability and Beirut's Post-War Reconstruction', *Development*, 54: 358–67. doi: 10.1057/dev.2011.53.

Badescu, G. (2019), 'Making Sense of Ruins: Architectural Reconstruction and Collective Memory in Belgrade', *Nationalities Papers*, 47 (2): 182–97.

Bassiki, M. and N. Mathiason (2021), 'Revealed: Syrians pay tax to rebuild after war but see little benefit', *Guardian*. Available at: https://www.theguardian.com/global-development/2021/may/24/revealed-syrians-pay-tax-to-rebuild-after-war-but-see-little-benefit.

BBC (2011), 'Syria Protests: Homs City Sit-in "Dispersed by Gunfire"', 19 April. Available online: https://www.bbc.com/news/world-middle-east-13130401 (accessed 6 December 2022).

Beall, J., T. Goodfellow and D. Rodgers (2013), 'Cities and Conflict in Fragile States in the Developing World', *Urban Studies*, 50 (15): 3065–83. doi: 10.1177/0042098013487775.

Beaujolais, A. (2016), *Qasef : Escaping the Bombing*. Available at: https://handicap-international.de/sn_uploads/de/document/study_qasef-syria-2016_web_finale.pdf (accessed 26 December 2022).

Bevan, R. (2006), *The Destruction of Memory: Architecture at War*, London: Reaktion Books.

Blunt, A. and R. Dowling (2006), *Home*, London: Routledge. doi: 10.4324/9780203401354.

Bou Akar, H. (2012), 'Contesting Beirut's Frontiers', *City and Society*. doi: 10.1111/j.1548-744X.2012.01073.x.

Bou Akar, H. (2019), *For the War Yet to Come: Planning Beirut's Frontier*, Stanford, CA: Stanford University Press.

Boym, S. (2001), *The Future of Nostalgia*, New York: Basic Books.

Brosché, J., M. Legnér, J. Kreutz and A. Ijla (2017), 'Heritage under Attack: Motives for Targeting Cultural Property during Armed Conflict', *International Journal of Heritage Studies*, 23 (3): 248–60. doi: 10.1080/13527258.2016.1261918.

Bsheer, R. (2017), 'Heritage as War', *International Journal of Middle East Studies*, 49 (4): 729–34. doi: 10.1017/S002074381700068X.

Bsheer, R. (2020), *Archive Wars*, Archive Wars, Stanford, CA: Stanford University Press. doi: 10.1515/9781503612587.

Bullock, N. (2002), *Building the Post-War World: Modern Architecture and Reconstruction in Britain*, London and New York: Routledge.

Bulos, N. (2020), 'The Beirut Blast Leveled Historic Neighborhoods: Some Fear Developers May Finish the Job', *Los Angeles Times*, 13 August. Available online: https://www.latimes.com/world-nation/story/2020-08-13/beirut-blast-leveled-historic-neighborhoods-fears-developers-destroy-more (accessed 26 December 2022).

Business 2 Business (2019), 'The Homs Governorate Says: The Homs Dream Project has Not been Canceled but We Will Amend It and Benefit from It!!', *Business 2 Business*. Available online: https://b2b-sy.com/news/55923/ (accessed 26 December 2022).

Calame, J. and E. Charlesworth (2011), *Divided Cities: Belfast, Beirut, Jerusalem, Mostar, and Nicosia*. doi: 10.5860/choice.47-3496.

Campbell, D., S. Graham and D. B. Monk (2007), 'Introduction to Urbicide: The Killing of Cities?', *Theory & Event*, 10 (2). doi: 10.1353/tae.2007.0055.

Catterall, B. (2014), 'Editorial: "City Makes Your Life Happier"', *City*, 18 (4–5): 381–5. doi: 10.1080/13604813.2014.964557.

Catterall, B. (2015), 'Editorial: To the City of Refuge', *City*, 19 (5): 613–17. doi: 10.1080/13604813.2015.1097080.

Channel 4 News (2018), *Death and Destruction in Yarmouk: Inside Syria's Largest Palestinian Refugee Camp*. Available online: https://www.youtube.com/watch?v=B1wXRuYTadI&t=439s (accessed 26 December 2022).

Chatty, D. (2017), 'The Syrian Humanitarian Disaster: Understanding Perceptions and Aspirations in Jordan, Lebanon and Turkey', *Global Policy*. doi: 10.1111/1758-5899.12390.

Chatty, D. (2018), *Syria: The Making and Unmaking of a Refuge State*, Oxford: Oxford University Press.

Cheung, F., A. Kube, L. Tay, E. Diener, J. J. Jackson, R. E. Lucas, M. Y. Ni and G. M. Leung (2020), 'The Impact of the Syrian Conflict on Population Well-Being', *Nature Communications*. doi: 10.1038/s41467-020-17369-0.

Chrisafis, A. (2013), 'Nazi Massacre Village Oradour-sur-Glane: Where Ghosts Must Live On', *Guardian*, 3 September. Available online: https://www.theguardian.com/world/2013/sep/03/oradour-sur-glane-nazi-massacre-village (accessed 26 December 2022).

Chulov, M. (2017), 'Iran Repopulates Syria with Shia Muslims to Help Tighten Regime's Control', *Guardian*, 13 January. Available online: https://www.theguardian.com/world/2017/jan/13/irans-syria-project-pushing-population-shifts-to-increase-influence (accessed 26 December 2022).

Clerc, V. (2014), 'Informal Settlements in the Syrian Conflict: Urban Planning as a Weapon', *Built Environment*, 40 (1): 34–51. doi: 10.2148/benv.40.1.34.

Coaffee, J. (2004), 'Rings of Steel, Rings of Concrete and Rings of Confidence: Designing out Terrorism in Central London Pre and Post September 11th', *International Journal of Urban and Regional Research*, 28 (1): 201–11. doi: 10.1111/j.0309-1317.2004.00511.x.

Coward, M. (2009) *Urbicide: The Politics of Urban Destruction*, London: Routledge. doi: 10.4324/9780203890639.

Cséfalvay, Z. (2011), 'Gated Communities for Security or Prestige? A Public Choice Approach and the Case of Budapest', *International Journal of Urban and Regional Research*, 35 (4): 735–52. doi: 10.1111/j.1468-2427.2010.00996.x.

Cusenza, C. (2019), 'Artists from Syria in the International Artworld: Mediators of a Universal Humanism', *Arts*, 8 (2): 45. doi: 10.3390/arts8020045.

Das, V. (2006), *Life and Words: Violence and the Descent into the Ordinary*, Berkeley and Los Angeles, CA: University of California Press.
De Cesari, C. and R. Dimova (2019), 'Heritage, Gentrification, Participation: Remaking Urban Landscapes in the Name of Culture and Historic Preservation', *International Journal of Heritage Studies*, 25 (9). doi: 10.1080/13527258.2018.1512515.
DiNapoli, E. K. (2019), 'Urbicide and Property under Assad: Examining Reconstruction and Neoliberal Authoritarianism in a "Postwar" Syria', *Columbia Human Rights Law Review*, 51 (1): 253–312.
Dillon, B. (2014a), *Ruin Lust*, London: Tate Gallery Publishing.
Dillon, B. (2014b), *Ruin Lust*, synopsis, London: Tate Gallery Publishing. Available online: https://www.amazon.co.uk/Ruin-Lust-Brian-Dillon/dp/1849763011 (accessed 26 December 2022).
Doderer, Y. P. (2011), 'LGBTQs in the City, Queering Urban Space', *International Journal of Urban and Regional Research*, 35 (2): 431–6. doi: 10.1111/j.1468-2427.2010.01030.x.
Doucet, L. (2013), 'Homs: War Changes the Soul of Syrian City', BBC, 25 January. Available online: https://www.bbc.com/news/world-21196409.
Elliott-Cooper, A., P. Hubbard and L. Lees (2020), 'Moving beyond Marcuse: Gentrification, Displacement and the Violence of Un-homing', *Progress in Human Geography*, 44 (3): 492–509. doi: 10.1177/0309132519830511.
Enab Baladi (2020), 'Hama Governor Orders Demolition of Residential Buildings under Pretext of Unlicensed Construction'. Available online: https://english.enabbaladi.net/archives/2020/12/hama-governor-orders-demolition-of-residential-buildings-under-pretext-of-unlicensed-construction/ (accessed 26 December 2022).
Fawaz, M. (2017), 'Exceptions and the Actually Existing Practice of Planning: Beirut (Lebanon) as Case Study', *Urban Studies*, 54 (8): 1938–55. doi: 10.1177/0042098016640453.
Fawaz, M., M. Harb and A. Gharbieh (2012), 'Living Beirut's Security Zones: An Investigation of the Modalities and Practice of Urban Security', *City and Society*, 24 (2): 173–95. doi: 10.1111/j.1548-744X.2012.01074.x.
Fine, S. (2020), 'Humanity at Night', *Aeon*. Available online: https://aeon.co/essays/in-times-of-crisis-the-arts-are-weapons-for-the-soul (accessed 26 December 2022).
Fox, K. (2017), 'The 13-Year-old Syrian Refugee who Became a Prizewinning Poet', *Guardian*, 1 October. Available online: https://www.theguardian.com/books/2017/oct/01/the-13-year-old-syrian-refugee-prizewinning-poet-amineh-abou-kerech-betjeman-prize (accessed 26 December 2022).
Fregonese, S. (2009), 'The Urbicide of Beirut? Geopolitics and the Built Environment in the Lebanese Civil War (1975–1976)', *Political Geography*, 28 (5): 309–18. doi: 10.1016/j.polgeo.2009.07.005.
Fried, M. (1970), 'Grieving for a Lost Home', in A. Kiev (ed.), *Social Psychiatry*, 335–59, London: Routledge. doi: 10.4324/9781315126197-20.
González Zarandona, J. A. and N. A. Munawar (2020), 'The Unfallen Statues of Hafez Al-Assad in Syria', *City*, 24 (3–4): 642–55. doi: 10.1080/13604813.2020.1784594.
Graham, S. (2009), 'Cities as Battlespace: The New Military Urbanism', *City*, 13 (4): 383–402. doi: 10.1080/13604810903298425.

Graham, S. (2018), 'Elite avenues', *City*, 22 (4): 527–50. doi: 10.1080/13604813.2017.1412190.
Grodach, C. (2002), 'Reconstituting Identity and History in Post-War Mostar, Bosnia-Herzegovina', *City*, 6 (1): 61–82. doi: 10.1080/13604810220142844.
Hafeda, M. (2019), *Negotiating Conflict in Lebanon: Bordering Practices in a Divided Beirut*, London: Bloomsbury Publishing.
Halasa, M., Z. Omareen and N. Mahfoud, eds (2014), *Syria Speaks: Art and Culture from the Frontline*. London: Saqi.
Halilovich, H. (2013), *Places of Pain: Forced Displacement, Popular Memory and Trans Local Identities in Bosnian War Torn Communities*, New York: Berghahn Books.
Harastani, N. and E. Hanna (2019), 'The Lateral Conflict of Urban Panning in Damascus', *Open House International*, 44 (2): 22–6.
Harb, M. (2016), 'Diversifying Urban Studies' Perspectives on the City at War', *International Journal of Urban and Regional Research*. Available online: https://www.ijurr.org/spotlight-on/the-city-at-war-reflections-on-beirut-brussels-and-beyond/diversifying-urban-studies-perspectives-on-the-city-at-war/ (accessed 26 December 2022).
Hardan, M. (2021), 'Russia Gains Foothold in Syria's Palmyra through Archaeological Restoration', *Al-Monitor*. Available online: https://www.al-monitor.com/originals/2021/06/russia-gains-foothold-syrias-palmyra-through-archaeological-restoration (accessed 26 December 2022).
Harrowell, E. (2016), 'Looking for the Future in the Rubble of Palmyra: Destruction, Reconstruction and Identity', *Geoforum*, 69: 81–3. doi: 10.1016/j.geoforum.2015.12.002.
Hårsman, B. and J. M. Quigley (1995), 'The Spatial Segregation of Ethnic and Demographic Groups: Comparative Evidence from Stockholm and San Francisco', *Journal of Urban Economics*, 37 (1): 1–16. doi: 10.1006/juec.1995.1001.
Harvey, D. (2008), 'The Right to the City', *New Left Review*. Available online: https://newleftreview.org/issues/ii53/articles/david-harvey-the-right-to-the-city (accessed 26 December 2022).
Hubbard, B. (2021), 'Fleeing a Modern War: Syrians Seek Refuge in Ancient Ruins', *New York Times*, 19 April. Available online: https://www.nytimes.com/2021/04/19/world/middleeast/fleeing-a-modern-war-syrians-seek-refuge-in-ancient-ruins.html (accessed 26 December 2022).
Hubbard, P., L. Faire and K. Lilley (2003), 'Contesting the Modern City: Reconstruction and Everyday Life in Post-War Coventry', *Planning Perspectives*, 18 (4): 377–97. doi: 10.1080/0266543032000117523.
Human Rights Watch (HRW) (2011), *'We Live as in War': Crackdown on Protesters in the Governorate of Homs, Syria*, 11 November. Available online: https://www.hrw.org/report/2011/11/11/we-live-war/crackdown-protesters-governorate-homs-syria (accessed 26 December 2022).
HRW (2014), *Razed to the Ground: Syria's Unlawful Neighborhood Demolitions in 2012–2013*, New York: Human Rights Watch.
HRW (2017), *Saudi Arabia: Security Forces Seal Off Eastern Town*, 13 August. Available online: https://www.hrw.org/news/2017/08/13/saudi-arabia-security-forces-seal-eastern-town# (accessed 26 December 2022).
HRW (2018), *Syria: Residents Blocked from Returning*, Human Rights Watch.

Available online: https://www.hrw.org/news/2018/10/16/syria-residents-blocked-returning (accessed 21 March 2020).
HRW (2019), *Rigging the System: Government Policies Co-Opt Aid and Reconstruction Funding in Syria*. Available online: https://www.hrw.org/sites/default/files/report_pdf/syria0619_web3.pdf (accessed 26 December 2022).
Imady, O. (2019), 'The Weaponization of Syria's Reconstruction', *Syria Studies*, 2 (1): 6–21. Available online: https://ojs.st-andrews.ac.uk/index.php/syria/article/view/1802 (accessed 26 December 2022).
Isakhan, B. and L. Meskell (2019), 'UNESCO's Project to "Revive the Spirit of Mosul": Iraq and Syrian Opinion on Heritage Reconstruction after the Islamic State', *International Journal of Heritage Studies*, 25 (11): 1189–1204. doi: 10.1080/13527258.2019.1578988.
Iskandarani, A. (2019), 'Using Instagram to Filter out Images of Conflict in Syria', *The National*. Available online: https://www.thenationalnews.com/arts-culture/art/using-instagram-to-filter-out-images-of-conflict-in-syria-1.932658 (accessed 26 December 2022).
Jaffe, R. (2017), 'The City at War: Reflections on Beirut, Brussels, and Beyond', *International Journal of Urban and Regional Research*. Available online: https://www.ijurr.org/spotlight-on/the-city-at-war-reflections-on-beirut-brussels-and-beyond/the-city-at-war/ (accessed 26 December 2022).
Jansen, S. and S. Löfving, eds (2009), *Struggles for Home: Violence, Hope and the Movement of People*, vol. 3, New York and Oxford: Berghahn Books.
Jansiz, G. (2014), 'Start Again: Let's Ditch Homs and Build a New One', *Royal Institute of British Architects Journal*. Available online: https://www.ribaj.com/culture/lets-build-a-new-homs (accessed 26 December 2022).
Jarrous, S. (2006), *A Homsi 'Videoclip': Souad Jarrous . . . The Arab Struggle*, *Voltaire Net*. Available online: https://www.voltairenet.org/article141874.html (accessed 5 December 2020).
Johnson, B. (2016), 'Bravo for Assad – He is a Vile Tyrant but He has Ssaved Palmyra from Isil', *The Telegraph*, 27 March.
Kaldor, M. and S. Sassen, eds (2020), *Cities at War: Global Insecurity and Urban Resistance*, New York: Columbia University Press.
Kanna, A. (2012), 'Urban Praxis and the Arab Spring', *City*, 16 (3): 360–8. doi: 10.1080/13604813.2012.687879.
Khalil, O. (2015), 'The People of the City: Unraveling the How in Ramlet Bulaq', *International Journal of Sociology*, 45 (3): 206–22. doi: 10.1080/00207659.2015.1066180.
Khalil, O. (2021), 'Cairo in Ten Years . . . Do We Know It?', *As-Safir Al-Arabi*. Available online: https://assafirarabi.com/ar/35568/2021/01/25/القاهرة-في-عشر-سنوات-هل-نعرفها/؟ (accessed 26 December 2022).
Khattab, A. and C. Cornish (2018), 'Threat of Syrian Home Demolitions Sparks Anger over Redevelopment', *Financial Times*, 9 December. Available online: https://www.ft.com/content/8b44a17c-e2ae-11e8-a6e5-792428919cee.
Lange-Maney, C. and J. Weier (2019), 'Cities as Feminist Spaces? Towards Experiments in Thinking and Living the Urban Differently', *City*, 23 (6): 808–10. doi: 10.1080/13604813.2020.1721163.
Larkin, C. (2010), 'Remaking Beirut: Contesting Memory, Space, and the Urban Imaginary of Lebanese Youth', *City & Community*, 9 (4): 414–42. doi: 10.1111/j.1540-6040.2010.01346.x.

Lopes de Souza, M. and B. Lipietz (2011), 'The "Arab Spring" and the City', *City*, 15 (6): 618–24. doi: 10.1080/13604813.2011.632900.

Loveless, J. (2013), 'Crisis in Lebanon: Camps for Syrian Refugees?', *Forced Migration Review*, 43: 66–8.

Loveluck, L. (2019), 'Syria is Ready to Court Investors, but Europe Wants to Prevent That', *Washington Post*, 23 January. Available online: https://www.washingtonpost.com/world/middle_east/syria-is-ready-to-court-investors-but-europe-wants-to-prevent-that/2019/01/23/a40abe52-1e4b-11e9-a759-2b8541bbbe20_story.html (accessed 26 December 2022).

Marcuse, P. (1993), 'What's so New about Divided Cities?', *International Journal of Urban and Regional Research*, 17 (3): 355–65. doi: 10.1111/j.1468-2427.1993.tb00226.x.

Marcuse, P. (2006), 'Security or Safety in Cities? The Threat of Terrorism after 9/11', *International Journal of Urban and Regional Research*, 30 (4): 919–29. doi: 10.1111/j.1468-2427.2006.00700.x.

Marques, E. (2015), 'Urban Poverty, Segregation and Social Networks in São Paulo and Salvador, Brazil', *International Journal of Urban and Regional Research*, 39 (6): 1067–83. doi: 10.1111/1468-2427.12300.

Mazur, K. (2020), 'Networks, Informal Governance, and Ethnic Violence in a Syrian City', *World Politics*, 72 (3): 481–524. doi: 10.1017/S0043887120000052.

MBC News (2019), *Inauguration of the Al Awamiyah's Centre Development Project*, video, YouTube, 30 January. Available online: https://www.youtube.com/watch?v=UpflVzJxmO0 (accessed 24 December 2022).

Mcfarlane, C. (2010), 'The Comparative City: Knowledge, Learning, Urbanism', *International Journal of Urban and Regional Research*, 34 (4): 725–42. doi: 10.1111/j.1468-2427.2010.00917.x.

Meskell, L. (2018), *A Future in Ruins: UNESCO, World Heritage, and the Dream of Peace*, Oxford: Oxford University Press.

Mizrokhi, E. (2021), 'Living in Anachronistic Space: Temporalities of Displacement in Moscow's Soviet-Era Standardised Housing', *Political Geography*, 91. doi: 10.1016/j.polgeo.2021.102495.

Mooney, E. (2014), 'The Inside Story: Internal Displacement in Syria', *Forced Migration Review*, 47.

Moore, R. (2020), 'How Syria's Blasted Landmarks are Starting to Rise from the Ruins', *Guardian*, 29 August. Available online: https://www.theguardian.com/artanddesign/2020/aug/29/how-syrias-blasted-cities-are-rising-from-the-ruins (accessed 26 December 2022).

Morrissey, M. and F. Gaffikin (2006), 'Planning for Peace in Contested Space', *International Journal of Urban and Regional Research*, 30 (4): 873–93. doi: 10.1111/j.1468-2427.2006.00696.x.

Munawar, N. A. (2017), 'Reconstructing Cultural Heritage in Conflict Zones: Should Palmyra be Rebuilt?', *EX NOVO Journal of Archaeology*, 2.

Murphy, K. (2016), 'Roger Michel', *New York Times*, 24 April. Available online: https://www.nytimes.com/2016/04/24/opinion/sunday/roger-michel.html?_r=0 (accessed 26 December 2022).

Nagel, C. (2002), 'Reconstructing Space, Re-creating Memory: Sectarian Politics and Urban Development in Post-War Beirut', *Political Geography*, 21 (5): 717–25. doi: 10.1016/S0962-6298(02)00017-3.

Nassar, A. (2021), 'With Government Complicity, Syrians' Property Falls Victim to Forgery', *Syria Direct*. Available online: https://syriadirect.org/with-government-complicity-syrians-property-falls-victim-to-forgery/ (accessed 26 December 2022).

Nixon, R. (2011). 'Slow Violence, Gender, and the Environmentalism of the Poor', in B. Caminero-Santangelo and G. Myers (eds), *Environment at the Margins: Literary and Environmental Studies in Africa*, 257–86, Athens, OH: Ohio University Press. doi: 10.1002/9781119118589.ch31.

Norwegian Refugee Council (2016), *Housing, Land and Property in the Syrian Arab Republic*, Oslo: Norwegian Refugee Council.

Ostrand, N. (2015), 'The Syrian Refugee Crisis: A Comparison of Responses by Germany, Sweden, the United Kingdom, and the United States', *Journal on Migration and Human Security*, 3 (3): 255–79. doi: 10.14240/jmhs.v3i3.51.

Othman, N. and R. Al-Jazaeri (2021), 'Reconstruction in Syria Should not be Linked to Political Conditions, Stepanov Says', SANA (Syrian Arab News Agency). Available online: https://sana.sy/en/?p=254009 (accessed 26 December 2022).

Park Residence Yaafour (2018), *Park Residence Yaafour*, video, YouTube. Available online: https://www.youtube.com/watch?v=y9B_wcdNLt0&t=2s (accessed 26 December 2022).

Piquard, B. and M. Swenarton (2011), 'Learning from Architecture and Conflict', *Journal of Architecture*, 16 (1): 1–13. doi: 10.1080/13602365.2011.557897.

Porteous, J. D. and S. E. Smith (2001), *Domicide: The Global Destruction of Home, McGill-Queen's Univesity Press*. Montreal: McGill-Queen's Press.

Proudfoot, P. (2017), 'The Smell of Blood: Accumulation by Dispossession, Resistance and the Language of Populist Uprising in Syria', *City*, 21 (3–4): 483–502. doi: 10.1080/13604813.2017.1331568.

Pullan, W. (2011), 'Frontier Urbanism: The Periphery at the Centre of Contested Cities', *Journal of Architecture*, 16 (1): 15–35. doi: 10.1080/13602365.2011.546999.

Pullan, W. and A. Azzouz (2019), 'Destruction and Reconstruction: How Urban Recovery has Become an Integral Part of Conflict and War', Centre for Urban Conflicts Research. Available online: https://www.urbanconflicts.arct.cam.ac.uk/downloads/briefing-paper-11-2019.pdf (accessed 26 December 2022).

Qaddour, J. (2020), 'Homs, a Divided Incarnation of Syria's Unresolved Conflict', in M. Yahya (ed.), *Contentious Politics in the Syrian Conflict: Opposition, Representation, and Resistance*, Beirut: Malcolm H. Kerr, Carnegie Middle East Centre, 15 May. Available online: https://carnegie-mec.org/2020/05/15/homs-divided-incarnation-of-syria-s-unresolved-conflict-pub-81804 (accessed 26 December 2022).

Qiblawi, T. (2017), 'Why Part of a Shia Town in Saudi Arabia has Been Flattened', CNN. Available at: https://edition.cnn.com/2017/08/12/middleeast/saudi-arabia-awamiya/index.html.

Qriema, S. (2021), 'The Consulate General of Iran Opened in Aleppo', SANA. Available online: https://sana.sy/en/?p=234038 (accessed 26 December 2022).

Rabbat, N. (2012), 'The Arab Revolution Takes Back the Public Space', *Critical Inquiry*, 39 (1): 198–208. doi: 10.1086/668055.

Rabbat, N. (2016), 'Syria's Past Can Be a Path to Its Future', *The Globe and Mail*.

Available online: https://www.theglobeandmail.com/opinion/syrias-past-can-be-a-path-to-its-future/article32555371/ (accessed 26 December 2022).

Radio and TV Station in Hama (2020), *Damage to Real Estate Documents in the Registry Department in Salamiyah as a Result of Water Leakage*, Facebook video, 4 February. Available online: https://fb.watch/9WRdmq8sl9/ (accessed 24 December 2022).

Rafea, M. (2019), 'Spaces of Masculinity', *aljumhuriya*. Available online: https://www.aljumhuriya.net/ar/content/فراغات-الرجولة (accessed 26 December 2022).

Rafea, M. (2021), 'We're Still Here', *aljumhuriya*. Available online: https://www.aljumhuriya.net/en/content/we're-still-here (accessed 26 December 2022).

Ragab, T. S. (2011), 'The Crisis of Cultural Identity in Rehabilitating Historic Beirut-Downtown', *Cities*, 28 (1): 107–14. doi: 10.1016/j.cities.2010.04.001.

Ramadan, A. (2009), 'Destroying Nahr el-Bared: Sovereignty and Urbicide in the Space of Exception', *Political Geography*, 28 (3): 153–63. doi: 10.1016/j.polgeo.2009.02.004.

Rasmussen, S. and N. Osseiran (2018), 'Out of Syria's Chaos, a Tycoon Builds a Fortune', *Wall Street Journal*. Available online: https://www.wsj.com/articles/out-of-syrias-chaos-a-tycoon-builds-a-fortune-1534100370 (accessed 26 December 2022).

Reuters (2019), 'US Sanctions Syrian Oligarch and His "Luxury Reconstruction Business Empire"', *Al Arabiya*, 11 June.

Riedlmayer, A. (2016), 'Erasing the Past: The Destruction of Libraries and Archives in Bosnia-Herzegovina', *Middle East Studies Association Bulletin*, 29 (1): 7–11. doi: 10.1017/s0026318400030418.

Rihani, W. (2020), 'Ten Minutes to Twelve', *aljumhuriya*. Available online: https://www.aljumhuriya.net/ar/content/الثانية-إلا-عشر-دقائق (accessed 26 December 2022).

Routledge, P. (2010), 'Introduction: Cities, Justice and Conflict', *Urban Studies*, 47 (6): 1165–77. doi: 10.1177/0042098009360240.

Sabbagh, H. (2016), 'China Ready to Work with Russia on Post-War Reconstruction in Syria', SANA. Available online: https://sana.sy/en/?p=75985 (accessed 26 December 2022).

Said, A. (2015), 'We Ought to Be Here: Historicizing Space and Mobilization in Tahrir Square', *International Sociology*, 30 (4): 348–66. doi: 10.1177/0268580914551306.

Said, S. and Yazigi, J. (2018), *The Reconstruction of Syria: Socially Just Re-integration and Peace Building or Regime Re-consolidation?*, Berlin: Friedrich-Ebert-Stiftung. Available online: https://books.google.co.uk/books/about/The_Reconstruction_of_Syria.html?id=nNTNzQEACAAJ&redir_esc=y/ (accessed 26 December 2022).

SANA (2019), 'President al-Assad: We Can Build Our Country Gradually, Gradually, and We Have Enough Human Resources, and Definitely China, Russia and Iran Will Have a Priority in the Reconstruction', SANA. Available online: https://sana.sy/en/?p=178025 (accessed 26 December 2022).

Sarkis, H. (2006), 'A Vital Void: Reconstructions in Downtown Beirut', in L. J. Vale and T. J. Campanella (eds), *The Resilient City: How Modern Cities Recover from Disaster*, 281–98, Oxford: Oxford University Press.

Sassin, S. (2017), 'When the Pursuit of National Security Produces Urban

Insecurity Cities', *International Journal of Urban and Regional Research*, 34: 15–24.

Sha, K. (2014), 'Destructive Construction and Constructive Conflicts', *Building Research & Information.*, 42 (3): 391–2.

Shahoud, Z. (2021), 'The Launch of the First Conference of Post-War Strategies and Experiences at Aleppo University', SANA. Available online: https://www.sana.sy/?p=1353974 (accessed 26 December 2022).

Smith, C., H. Burke, C. de Leiuen and G. Jackson (2016), 'The Islamic State's Symbolic War: Da'esh's Socially Mediated Terrorism as a Threat to Cultural Heritage', *Journal of Social Archaeology*, 16 (2): . doi: 10.1177/1469605315617048.

Solnit, R. (2016), *Hope in the Dark: Untold Histories, Wild Possibilities*. Chicago, IL: Haymarket Books. doi: 10.1215/9781478007135-086.

Sukarieh, M. and S. Tannock (2018), 'Subcontracting Academia: Alienation, Exploitation and Disillusionment in the UK Overseas Syrian Refugee Research Industry', *Antipode*, 51 (2): 664–80. doi: 10.1111/anti.12502.

Sulaiman, B. (2019), 'In Appreciation of Their Sacrifices . . . A Memorial to the Martyrs in Sankari', *Al Oruba*. Available online: http://ouruba.alwehda.gov.sy/homs-news/71519 (accessed 2022).

Tahdir4Syria (2017), *A Letter from Dr Bassma Kodmani*, Arab Reform Initiative (ARI), video, Facebook, 18 January. Available online: https://www.facebook.com/Tahdir4Syria/videos/1926973847522765/ (accessed 26 December 2022).

Tate Modern (2021), *Shirin Neshat Explores the Themes of Exile, Identity and Cultural History in This Video Installation*, Tate Modern. Available online: https://www.tate.org.uk/visit/tate-modern/display/shirin-neshat (accessed 26 December 2022).

Tedong, P. A., J. L. Grant and W. N. A. Wan Abd Aziz (2015), 'Governing Enclosure: The Role of Governance in Producing Gated Communities and Guarded Neighborhoods in Malaysia', *International Journal of Urban and Regional Research*, 39 (1): 112–28. doi: 10.1111/1468-2427.12204.

The Economist (2016), 'A Russian Orchestra Plays Bach and Prokofiev in the Ruins of Palmyra', 6 May. Available online: https://www.economist.com/europe/2016/05/06/a-russian-orchestra-plays-bach-and-prokofiev-in-the-ruins-of-palmyra (accessed 26 December 2022).

The New Arab and agencies (2017), 'Violence Erupts Following Saudi Demolition of Historic Shia Homes', *The New Arab*. Available online: https://english.alaraby.co.uk/english/news/2017/6/27/violence-erupts-following-saudi-demolition-of-historic-shia-homes (accessed 26 December 2022).

The Syria Report (2020), 'Explained: Informal Settlements, Between Laws of Development and Urban Planning', November. Available online: https://hlp.syria-report.com/hlp/explained-informal-settlements-between-laws-of-development-and-urban-planning/ (accessed 26 December 2022).

The Syria Report (2021a), 'Business Owners in Old Homs Forced to Open Shop or Face Confiscation'. Available online: https://hlp.syria-report.com/hlp/business-owners-in-old-homs-forced-to-open-shop-or-face-confiscation/ (accessed 26 December 2022).

The Syria Report (2021b), 'Explained: Informal Housing in Hama'. Available online: https://hlp.syria-report.com/hlp/explained-informal-housing-in-hama/ (accessed 26 December 2022).

Thompson, E. L. (2017), 'Legal and Ethical Considerations for Digital Recreations of Cultural Heritage', *Chapman Law Review*, 20 (1): 153–76.
Tuathail, G. and C. Dahlman (2006), 'Post-Ddomicide Bosnia and Herzegovina: Homes, Homelands and One Million Returns', *International Peacekeeping*, 13 (2): 242–60. doi: 10.1080/13533310500437647.
UN-Habitat (2013), *Urban Syria*, Damascus. Available online: https://mirror.unhabitat.org/downloads/docs/UrbanSnapshots2.pdf (accessed 26 December 2022).
UN-Habitat (2014), 'City Profile Homs: Multi Sector Assessment'. Available online: https://www.alnap.org/system/files/content/resource/files/main/Homs%20RCP.pdf (accessed 26 December 2022).
UN Human Rights (2017), *Saudi Arabia's Use of Force and Demolitions in the Al-Masora Neighborhood Violates Human Rights: Destruction of Al-Masora*, Geneva: United Nations, 24 May. Available online: https://www.ohchr.org/en/NewsEvents/Pages/DisplayNews.aspx?NewsID=21657&LangID=E (accessed 26 December 2022).
United Nations Educational, Scientific and Cultural Organization (UNESCO) (n.d.), *UNESCO-EU: Launch of the Emergency Safeguarding of the Syrian Heritage project*, UNESCO. Available online: http://www.unesco.org/new/en/safeguarding-syrian-cultural-heritage/international-initiatives/emergency-safeguarding-of-syria-heritage/ (accessed 1 May 2018).
United Nations High Commissioner for Refugees (UNHCR) (2017), *In Syria's Homs, UNHCR Syria Representative Meets with Returnees*, UNHCR. Available online: http://www.unhcr.org/sy/10917-syrias-homs-unhcr-syria-representative-meets-returnees.html (accessed 1 May 2018).
Unruh, J. D. (2016), 'Weaponization of the Land and Property Rights System in the Syrian Civil War: Facilitating Restitution?', *Journal of Intervention and Statebuilding*, 10 (4): 453–71. doi: 10.1080/17502977.2016.1158527.
Vale, L. J. (2014), 'The Politics of Resilient Cities: Whose Resilience and Whose City?', *Building Research and Information*, 42 (2): 191–201. doi: 10.1080/09613218.2014.850602.
Viejo-Rose, D. (2011), *Reconstructing Spain Cultural Heritage and Memory After Civil War*, Chicago, IL: Sussex Academic Press.
Vignal, L. (2014), 'Destruction-in-Progress: Revolution, Repression and War Planning in Syria (2011 Onwards)', *Built Environment*, 40 (3): 326–41. doi: 10.2148/benv.40.3.326.
Vignal, L. (2016), 'Dubai on Barada? The Making of "Globalized Damascus" in Times of Urban Crisis', in S. Wippel, K. Bromber, C. Steiner and B. Krawietz (eds), *Under Construction: Logics of Urbanism in the Gulf Region*, 259–70, Abingdon: Routledge. doi: 10.4324/9781315549323-36.
Webb, M. S. (2018), 'Local Responses to the Protection of Medieval Buildings and Archaeology in British Post-War Town Reconstruction: Southampton and Coventry', *Urban History*, 45 (4): 635–59. doi: 10.1017/S0963926818000019.
Wollentz, G. (2017), 'Making a Home in Mostar: Heritage and the Temporalities of Belonging', *International Journal of Heritage Studies*, 23 (10): 928–45. doi: 10.1080/13527258.2017.1347891.
World Bank (2019), *The World Bank in Syrian Arab Republic*. Available online: http://www.worldbank.org/en/country/syria/overview (accessed 26 December 2022).

Wu, F. and C.-P. Pow (2010), 'Reviews: Gated Communities in China: Class, Privilege and the Moral Politics of the Good Life, Developing China: Land, Politics and Social Conditions', *Environment and Planning A: Economy and Space*, 42 (7): 1762–5. doi: 10.1068/a4207rvw.

Yazigi, J. (2017), *Destruct to Reconstruct: How the Syrian Regime Capitalises on Property Destruction and Land Legislation*, Berlin: Friedrich-Ebert-Stifung. Available online: https://library.fes.de/pdf-files/iez/13562.pdf.

Zaidi, S. (2020), 'Homing and Unhoming: Taxonomies of Living', *Chiragh Dilli*. Available online: https://chiraghdilli.com/2020/08/07/homing-and-unhoming-taxonomies-of-living/ (accessed 26 December 2022).

Zaman al Wsl (2007), 'Between the Officials and Brokers, the Homs Dream Crawls over the Dreams of the Poor', *Zaman al Wsl*. Available online: https://www.zamanalwsl.net/news/article/2343 (accessed 26 December 2022).

Zamanalwsl (2007), 'The Homs Dream: All the Details with Images', *Zamanalwsl*. Available online: https://www.zamanalwsl.net/news/article/2612/ (accessed 26 December 2022).

Zhang, Y. (2014) *The Vulnerable Observer: Fear, Sufferings and Boundary Crossing*, *Field Research Method Lab Blog LSE*, London: LSE Blogs. Available online: https://blogs.lse.ac.uk/fieldresearch/2014/04/04/the-vulnerable-observer/ (accessed 26 December 2022).

Zhang, Y. (2015) 'Squatting to End Domicide? Resisting Bulldozer Urbanism in Contemporary Shanghai', *Erde*, 146 (2–3): 139–50. doi: 10.12854/erde-146-12.

Zhang, Y. (2017a), 'Family or Money? The False Dilemma in Property Dispossession in Shanghai', *International Journal of Urban and Regional Research*, 41 (2): 194–212. doi: 10.1111/1468-2427.12455.

Zhang, Y. (2017b), '"It Felt Like You Were at War": State of Exception and Wounded Life in the Shanghai Expo-Induced Domicide', in K. Brickell, M. Fernández Arrigoitia and A. Vasudevan (eds), *Geographies of Forced Eviction: Dispossession, Violence, Resistance*, 97–119, London: Palgrave Macmillan. doi: 10.1057/978-1-137-51127-0_5.

Zhang, Y. (2018), 'Domicide, Social Suffering and Symbolic Violence in Contemporary Shanghai, China', *Urban Geography*, 39 (2): 190–213. doi: 10.1080/02723638.2017.1298978.

Ziada, H. (2015), 'What Brings them There? Reflections on the Persisting Symbolism of Tahrir Square', *Jadaliyya*. Available online: https://www.jadaliyya.com/Details/31939 (accessed 26 December 2022).

Index

Note: Page references in *italic* refer to figures and those in **bold** refer to tables

31 Days in the Capital of Revolution (Chung) 90–2, *91*

Akar, Hiba Bou 54, 135
Al-Baath University 41–3
Al Basil High School for Outstanding Students 40
Al Ghassaniah Orthodox School 40
alienation
    due to loss of home 68
    space of 52–3
Al-Jumhuriya (platform) 104, 127
Amnesty International 9, 24–5
Arab Reform Initiative (ARI) 103
Arab Spring 9, 10, 44, 45, 47, 90
Arab Urbanism 132
Arafa, Amal 6
architects
    communities and 41–4
    'everyone is an architect' 75–6
    at the time of war 73–5
Architectural Association (AA) 9
artists 85, 96, 34
    local charities working with 72
    responses to domicide 89–92
    Soubhi Shoaib Fine Art, as destination for 34
Asali, Wesam Al 13, 133
Atkinson, Rowland 68

Baba Amr 52
Barazi, Talal 120
Basateen El-Razi 110–11
The Battle for Home: Memoir of a Syrian Architect (Al-Sabouni) 31, 73
Bennoune, Karima 21
Berlin Wall 8, 23, 86

Bevan, Robert 53
Blunt, Alison 15–16
Bokova, Irina 10
Boym, Svetlana 79–80
Bsheer, Rosie 5, 11, 120
Building for Hope: Towards an Architecture of Belonging (Al-Sabouni) 73

Catterall, Bob 15
charities 14, 24–6, 52–3, 77, 121
    as collective act of solidarity 71–2
    rehabilitation work conducted by 69–70
Chatty, Dawn 83–4, 87–8, 128–9
Chen Xiaodong 116
Chung, Tiffany 90–2
Civil War of 1975–1990 54, 86, 123
Clerc, Valérie 54, 113
Clock Tower Square 44–9, *45*, 60, 81, *82*, 120–1
collective spaces of solidarity 131–4
Council for At-Risk Academics (CARA) 43
Coventry of the Future exhibition 98
Coward, Martin 6
Creative Memory of the Syrian Revolution 84
cultural heritage 104, 117–22
    attention and outrage due to destruction of 10
    creation of protection zones 11
    destruction 11, 19, 20, 33, 51, 52, 84, 95
    reconstructing 117–22
    targeted 5
Culture in Crisis programme 10

INDEX

Damascus 5, 22, 31, 37, 111, 114, 131.
See also Hama
   outrage in Marota City 110
   reports announced by residents of 58
   siege laid by Syrian government 51
   Yarmouk Camp 66
Darwish, Mahmoud 67
Das, Veena 14
The Day After (TDA) 3, 113
Deir ez-Zur 9
Department of Architecture, Homs, Syria 41–3
Destruction of Memory: Architecture at the time of war (Bevan) 53
The Destruction of the City of Homs (Petherbridge) 93–5
Dillon, Brian 87
displacement 2–3, 19, 26, 53, 56, 58, 62–3. *See* internally displaced persons (IDPs)
   anthropology and refugee studies 16
   destruction and 22, 25, 35, 69, 72, 73, 74, 88, 106, 116, 136
   dispossession and 38
   disruption of interpersonal networks 80
   forced 16, 53, 77, 79, 83, 95, 104, 111
   governments justifying demolitions of buildings 36
   impacted communities research 11
   oppression of academics and 43
Domicide: The Global Destruction of Home (Porteous and Smith) 18
Dowling, Robyn 15–16

Elite Avenues (Graham) 36
Emam, Tameem 103
Enab Baladi (non-profit media) 114
Endangered Archaeology 10
Epigraph, Damascus (Mehretu) 90
everyday domicide 18–19
exclusion 17, 36, 40
extreme domicide 18–19

Faire, L. 98
Fairouz 35

Fakhani, Hani 13
Fine, Sarah 96
For Sama (film) 51
For the War Yet to Come (Akar) 135
A Future in Ruins: UNESCO, World Heritage, and the Dream of Peace (Meskell) 10–11
The Future of Nostalgia (Boym) 79–80

Gaffikin, Frank 41
Gaza 9
gentrification 32, 68
Ghazal, Mohammed Iyad 36, 37, 44
Graham, Stephen 36
grey layer 49
Guardian 121

Haddad, Kurjeyah 48
Hafeda, Mohamad 50
Haj Saleh, Yassin al- 40
Halilovich, Hariz 83
Hama 2–5, *4*, 19, 58, 104, 114, 123. *See also* Damascus
Harb, Mona 9
Harvey, David 46
Heritage as War (Bsheer) 11
Hezbollah 1–2
Hiroshima Prefectural Industrial Promotional Hall 86
Home (Dowling and Blunt) 15–16
Homs 29, *32*, *33*, *63–66*
   demolition of the Soubhi Shoaib Fine Art Centre 34–5
   'Development and Modernization' movement 39
   government justifying demolitions of buildings 36
   growth of migrants in 31
   growth of racial and class segregation in 41
   history 32–3
   New Clock Square 44–9, *45*, 60, 81, *82*
   protests 37–8, 44, *46*
   sense of exile and strangerness 54
   'The Homs Dream' project 36
   urban growth in 30, 31
   urban life inside 125–7
   urban planning in 30, 31, 37

INDEX

use of stones in architecture 30
violence against its built environment 34
Homs City Council 107
Homs Dream project 36–8, 42, 44, 46, 76, 107, 120
Hope in the Dark: Untold Histories, Wild Possibilities (Solnit) 127
Housing, Land and Property (HLP) 1, 2, 115
    documents of displaced people 113
    research on 3
Hubbard, P. 98
Human Rights Watch (HRW) 3, 24, 58, 114

identity 14–17, 53, 80, 94, 99, 121, 134
    cultural 85
    ethnic 7
    of forcibly displaced 83
    legal 113
    space of 8, 20, 30–6
The Impossible Revolution: Making Sense of the Syrian Tragedy (al-Haj Saleh) 40
inequality, space of 36–41
Institute for Digital Archaeology (IDA) 121
internal displacement, impact on people 61–9. *See also* displacement
Internal Displacement Monitoring Centre 56
internally displaced persons (IDPs) 2–3, 25–6, 51, 56–61, 70, 77, 92, 109. *See also* displacement
    impact on 61–9
International University for Science and Technology (IUST) 75
Iraq 1, 6, 9, 11, 51, 88, 99, 104, 133
Iraqi Women Academics Network (IWAN) 133
Islamic State of Iraq and the Levant (ISIS) 5, 11, 89, 121

Jamiat Al-Bir wa Al-Khadamat Al-Ejtemae a (Charity of Righteousness and Social Services) 69, 70
Jansen, Stef 16
Jansiz, Ghassan 107
Jarrous, Souad 34
Johnson, Boris 89
Joukhadar, Farah 34
Jwadi, Houda 13

Kaixun Sha 20
Karman, Maher 116
Khalid ibn al-Walid Mosque 45, 117, 118
Khalil, O. 20
Kodmani, B. 103
Krishati, M. 114

Libya 6, 9, 45, 129, 131
Life and Words: Violence and the Descendent into the Ordinary (Das) 14
Lilley, K. 98
Löfving, S. 16

Maktoum, Sheikh Mohammed bin Rashid Al 122
Marini, Philippe 36
Marota City 106, 110–11, 114
Masha' al-Arb'een 3–5, 114
Masri, Emad Al 13, 31
Mehretu, Julie 90
Mekdad, Faisal 116
Meskell, Lyn 10–11
Michel, Roger 122
Ministry of Local Administration (MoLA) 61
Misrata 9
Mizrokhi, Ekaterina 35
Morrissey, Mike 41
Mosul 9
Mousalli, Shahd 103
Municipal Administration Modernization (MAM) 31

Negotiating Conflict in Lebanon: Bordering Practices in Divided Beirut (Hafeda) 50
Neshat, Shirin 80–1
New York Times 122
Nimr, Ameen al- 21
Nixon, Rob 29, 126

INDEX

North Atlantic Treaty Organization (NATO) 10
Norwegian Refugee Council 3
Nuri Mosque 44

Oday, Umm 3

Park Residence Yaafour 108, 109, 110
peacetime domicide 20–2
Petherbridge, D. 93–5, 134
Places of Pain (Halilovich) 83
Polish School of Architecture 131
Porteous, J. Douglas 14, 15, 18, 62
protests 21, 37–38, 44–8, **49**, 90, 121

Qatari Solidere 36

Rabbat, N. 47–8, 115
Raqqa 9, 131
Razed to the Ground: Syria's Unlawful Neighborhood Demolitions in 2012–2013 3, 58, 114
Reconstructing Spain: Cultural Heritage and Memory after Civil War (Viejo-Rose) 97
Reconstruction as Violence (symposium) 115
representation 79–96
  artists' responses to domicide 89–92
  Syria in exile 79–89
resisting domicide 127–31
Rethink Rebuild Society 84
Rihani, Wael 47
Ruin Lust (Dillon) 87

Sabouni, Marwa Al- 13, 31, 73
Saja, Hiba Al 31
Sassin, Saskia 7
Sebai, Taher Al 43
Shaaban, Bouthaina (doctor) 116
shabiha (state-sponsored militias) 126
Sharp, D. 115
Shia Muslims 21
slow violence 19, 26, 29, 54
Slow Violence and the Environmentalism of the Poor (Nixon) 29
Smith, Sandra E. 14, 15, 18, 62

solidarity 96, 128
  charities as collective act of 71–2
  collective spaces of 131–4
  Syrians and international artists 89
  urban scholarly activism 34
Soliloquy (Neshat) 80–1
Solnit, Rebecca 127
Start Again: Let's Ditch Homs and Build a New One (Jansiz) 107
Stepanov, Oleg 117
Struggles for Home: Violence, Hope and the Movement of People (Jansen and Löfving) 16
Sunni 40, 49, 73, 119
Syrian Arts and Culture Festival (SACF) 84
Syrian Reconstruction Committee 116
The Syria Project 13, 90–2, 103, 132
Syria: The Making and Unmaking of a Refuge State (Chatty) 83–4

Tahrir Square 44, 47–8
Taiz 9
Thomson, Alex 64
Touma, Tarek 90

Um Al Zennar Church 119
UN-Habitat's City Profile Homs 59
United Nations Development Programme (UNDP) 69, 118
United Nations Educational, Scientific and Cultural Organization (UNESCO) 10
United Nations High Commissioner for Refugees (UNHCR) 69, 92, 118
Unruh, Jon D. 115
Urbegony 133
Urbicide: The Politics of Urban Destruction (Coward) 6

Victoria and Albert Museum (V&A) 10
Viejo-Rose, Dacia 97
Vignal, Leïla 108

INDEX

Walid, Khalid ibn a - 30
Wathiqat Wattan 6

Xie Xiaoyan 116

Yarmouk Camp 64, 66–8
Yazigi, Jihad 1
Yemen 6
Yunpeng Zhang 15, 17–18

Zaher, Mohammed Al 21
Zahrawi, Naeem Salim
    Al- 31
Zaidi, Sarover 77
Zainedin, Sawsan Abou 13,
    104
Zankawan, Omama 18, 56–7
Zarif, Mohammad Javad 116
Zhang, Yunpeng 136